JELLY SHOT
TEST KITCHEN
Jell-ing Classic Cocktails—
ONE DRINK AT A TIME

JELLY SHOT
TEST KITCHEN

Jell-ing Classic Cocktails—
ONE DRINK AT A TIME

by MICHELLE PALM

Photography by Amy Webster & Michelle Palm

Running Press

PHILADELPHIA · LONDON

This book is dedicated to
my amazing husband, Jeff, and stepson, Devin.

Thanks for your love, patience and support, for always opening
the refrigerator door very carefully, and for never complaining
when the milk was hidden behind a maze of jelly shots. XOXOX

Library of Congress Control Number: 2010942877
ISBN 978-0-7624-4054-2

Cover and interior design by Frances J. Soo Ping Chow
Edited by Jennifer Kasius
Typography: Berthold Akzidenz Grotesk, Brownstone
Sans, Helvetica Neue, and Suburban

Running Press Book Publishers
2300 Chestnut Street
Philadelphia, PA 19103-4371

Visit us on the web!
www.runningpress.com

TABLE OF CONTENTS

Introduction

WE HAVE ALWAYS loved gelatin, from plain and simple dessert cups and jigglers to the multilayered and textured jello 1-2-3, to fancy molded-gelatin extravaganzas dotted with fruit, nuts, and mini-marshmallows. Particularly for those of us who grew up before pre-made gelatin desserts were available in every supermarket, gelatin held a somewhat magical allure. Just think about it: Via an alchemic combination of hot and cold water and a little time in the refrigerator, a packet of pastel powder becomes a solid, wiggly, and, well, downright friendly-seeming dessert! Post formative years, we also enjoyed that merger of gelatin and alcohol known as the jello shot, which, potency aside, is just plain fun!

It was no surprise then, when Michelle wondered if jello shots might be a fun addition to the menu for a small backyard party. Given the guest list, these could not be the typical, paper-cup-clad vodka-spiked shooters. Rather, she was aiming for a more sophisticated specimen, a translation of a cocktail. Initial Internet searches were discouraging, yielding mostly recipes for jello shots that, although sporting a cocktail name, were based on a flavored gelatin. (Think: "Mojito" shots made with lime jello, rum, and chopped mint leaves. *That's no Mojito!*) Finally, amid mentions of gelatin cocktails served at high-end bars and restaurants, she stumbled upon a gorgeous *Los Angeles Times* piece featuring "real" gelatin cocktails presented *sans* Dixie cups or other containment. Recipes were included in the article, but the recipes called for sheet gelatin, which was not readily available in our area.

Inspired, Michelle rolled up her sleeves and decided to create original recipes, using ingredients available at the local supermarket and liquor store. The first attempts, Piña Colada and Cosmopolitan jelly shots, prepared using the classic formulations for each cocktail and garnished simply, were the hit of the party. Friends clamored for more recipes, followed by challenges—can you make a Long Island? A Margarita? The next jelly shots off the blocks, including Tequila Sunrise, Baileys & Coffee, and Apple Martini jelly shots, took a bit of tweaking to reach their final form, but given the enthusiastic feedback for each, spurred Michelle on to gelatinize other cocktail favorites.

The moment when the Jelly Shot Test Kitchen concept really took off, however, is when Michelle's siter Amy, an avid photographer, snapped a few photos of the Jelly Shots to illustrate the blog (http://jelly-shot-test-kitchen.blogspot.com). Michelle had started to keep friends and family current on new arrivals to the Halls of Gelatin. Amy's gorgeous pictures inspired us to take the project to the next level: A few months later, we had a bundle of recipes, a burgeoning photo album, and a publishing contract . . .

Why call them jelly shots, you might ask. Aren't jelly shots basically just a jello shot? While the jello shot was undeniably the springboard for the concept, the differences in ingredients and presentation set the jelly shot apart from its college-days cousin. "Jelly shot" is a term already in use in the culinary community as a descriptor for gelatin cocktails, along with several variations using the French geleé. Additionally, the terms "jelly shot," or "vodka jelly," are also more commonly used in many parts of the world.

In the following pages, we present our gelatin interpretations of 68 classic and popular cocktail recipes (okay, 66 plus two of our own twists on a theme), as well as eight alcohol-free "mocktail" jelly shots perfect for any of your guests who are unable imbibe for various reasons and would enjoy a non-boozy alternative to the full-octane jelly shots.

The jelly shots were translated directly from the cocktail recipes into gelatin form wherever possible, using classic proportions of alcohol to mixers. Accuracy was important—one could say that we are as passionate about recreating classic cocktails as we are about drinking them. (Others might imply that we are a touch OCD. We can't argue there, only point out that this is a topic best left for another time). Throughout our gelatin adventures, we did occasionally run across cocktails that needed a tweak here and there in order to arrive at a palatable jelly shot. Take the Lemon Drop jelly shot, for example. Made to the exact cocktail proportions, in gelatin form this recipe could, quite frankly, clean your windows.

Our interpretation of the Lemon Drop therefore includes a subtle mixer—and the result is just as lemony and potent as its cocktail inspiration, without harming itself or others. With that in mind, don't be alarmed when, from time to time, water is added where there is none in the original cocktail recipe, or perhaps there is a slightly higher ratio of mixers used than expected. (For one thing, the gelatin needs a certain amount of water in order to set.) Trust that the end result of the recipe is in keeping with the original spirit of the cocktail, or it wouldn't be in the book. *(Blast you, Sazerac cocktail and your non-gelatinizing ways!)*

Whatever the recipe, cocktails ARE extremely personal. Feel free to experiment with your own jelly shots, mixing them to your taste just as you would with your cocktails. Want to tone down your Margarita jelly shot a notch? Try a little water or lime juice in place of some tequila. Want more Cointreau? Just add a bit and cut back the tequila. You will always be okay swapping out a little of one alcohol for another, or adding more mixer and less alcohol.

Finally, we hope you enjoy the photos and recipes in this book, and that jelly shots bring as much fun and frivolity to your gatherings as they have to ours.

Cheers,
Michelle & Amy, *Jelly Shot Test Kitchen*

A Brief History

OF JELLY SHOTS

A little culinary research reveals that the ancestors of the jelly shot trace back to the high art of Parisian *haute cuisine* as it was emerging in the early 1800s, when Antonin Carême, the baker of Napoleon Bonaparte's wedding cake, recorded a contemporary recipe for "Orange-Flower and Pink Champagne Jelly." Carême's Champagne jelly calls for sugar and water to be combined with orange blossoms, then mixed with isinglass (a natural form of gelatin) and rosé Champagne. Adding cochineal (a red dye) to the partially set jelly produced a pink marbled effect. At the time, the concept of a savory, rather than a sweet, aspic or gelatin was a regular accompaniment to formal meals and was likely an expected item on such an elaborate, multi-course menu.

The next notable reference is a recipe for "Punch Jelly" which appeared in Jerry Thomas's *How To Mix Drinks or The Bon Vivant's Companion*, the classic 1860s barkeep's guide. Punch Jelly calls for a strong Punch à la Ford (cognac and rum sweetened with sugar and lemons) to be gelled. Obviously no stranger to good times, Mr. Thomas included an important admonition regarding the recipe: *"Punch Jelly is a very insinuating and deceptive refreshment, because its strength is not appreciated when partaking of it, and it must therefore be indulged in with becoming moderation."* Advice still apt for the modern imbiber.

The gelatin cocktail scene then grows mysteriously quiet until the 1950s appearance of the now ubiquitous jello shot. This rendition of the alcoholic gelée was a pop culture, Everyman's combination of fruit-flavored gelatin spiked with a high-proof spirit, typically vodka. Although it's difficult to pinpoint a specific origin, the most entertaining mythology surrounding the birth of the jello shot involves a mathematician, a military base, and contraband. Tom Lehrer, an American satirist, musician, and mathematician, is somewhat seriously credited with the first intentional production of the jello shot as a party favor.

In an interview with the *San Francisco Weekly*, Mr. Lehrer recounts the genesis this way: "What happened was, I was in the Army for two years, and we were having a Christmas party on the naval base where I was working in Washington, D.C. The rules said no alcoholic beverages were allowed. And we wanted to have a little party, so this friend and I spent an evening experimenting with jello. It wasn't a beverage." After a bit of experimentation (and presumably some taste-testing) the best combination was settled at: orange jello and vodka in Dixie cups. Whipped cream garnish, it seems, had not yet made an appearance on the scene.

How then, did the spirited gelée, a little nibble with such aristocratic origins, fall from grace to languish temporarily in the halls of college mixers and black-label spirits? Our theory? We blame its vestiment, the Dixie cup. Now don't get us wrong—it's not as if we've never had a jello shot in a Dixie cup. On the contrary! No one can argue the contagious fun of a jiggly cocktail, but given the limited number of appropriate social venues for a Dixie cup (and we challenge you to name five), a Dixie cup-clad gelatin cocktail will likely fare no better. While the root cause of the downfall is unclear, thankfully restoration is in sight. In the early 1990s, a new era of experimental cuisine began to emerge. A spirit of pushing the envelope of traditional conventions was on the horizon. The new name of the culinary game became unexpected flavor combinations, dishes deconstructed, twisted, turned inside out, and savory flavors where you would expect to find sweet. This was around the time when the Iron Chefs on the original cult-hit TV cooking contest would typically power up the ice cream maker to churn a batch of, yes, sardine gelato.

Pescetarian dairy sweets aside, with all this experimentation, it was only a matter of time before cocktails began to change shape as well. Sips such as The Proud Mary, which is served at the molecular-gastronomy Mecca WD-50 in New York, feature horseradish-infused vodka, celery bitters, and a workflow including a carbonation process and gelling compounds to clarify solids. The end result, described in an article in the *The Wall Street Journal*, is the sparkling wine version of a ho-hum Bloody Mary. In the same *Wall Street Journal* article, chef Grant Achatz of Chicago's award-winning Alinea restaurant describes his geléed version of the Sazerac cocktail as "the size of a thimble . . . [with] all the classic components of a Sazerac. But you're chewing and it's fun." At The Fat Duck, a Michelin three-star restaurant in Berkshire, England, Whiskey Wine Gums infused with different varieties of Scotch are served on a corresponding map of Scotland.

"Is it a foam, a food, or a drink?" asks The Art of Drink, a popular cocktail Website. "Is a Jelly Shot a bite or a beverage?" We're still pondering that one, too. The topic is best reserved for a good philosophical discussion to be savored with an Old Fashioned (liquid or solid) in hand. Whatever name you call them by, jelly shots and their siblings in the mixology family have hit the big time.

Amid all the fascinating culinary experimentation, a challenge for the home chef remains. Molecular gastronomy is known for its dependence on a laboratory-like environment filled with liquid nitrogen, blow torches, *sous vide* low-temperature cooking, food dehydrators, dry ice, obscure chemical compounds to turn liquids into solid caviar-shaped drops, smoke and mirrors, and a kitchen full of staff. The jelly shot recipes in this cookbook bring it all down to size for the rest of us, elevating the jelly shot from the Dixie cup to a refined, delicious, edible cocktail.

BEFORE YOU START:
A NOTE ON INGREDIENTS AND MEASURES

W e wrote and tested the recipes in this book using packets of pre-measured Knox-brand granulated gelatin, which are readily available at most supermarkets in the U.S. For those in the U.K., where leaf gelatin is more commonly used, we found that it substituted just fine, according to the measures listed below. In the *Jelly Shot Test Kitchen*, Dr. Oetker Gold extra gelatine sheets produced the best texture.

You can also refer to this handy chart for exact measures for recipes that call for dividing a packet of Knox pre-measured gelatin powder.

1 envelope Knox gelatin = 2¼ teaspoons gelatin powder = 3½ sheets Dr. Oetker Gold extra
½ envelope Knox gelatin = about 1 teaspoon gelatin powder = 1¾ sheets Dr. Oetker Gold extra

* * *

ARE YOU VEGETARIAN?

Just because you don't eat animal products doesn't mean you can't join in on the fun. Agar-agar powder is available at most grocery stores, and are a good vegan alternative to gelatin.

1 packet Knox = ½ teaspoon agar-agar powder

First, make sure all your ingredients are at room temperature. Add ½ of your mixer liquids (i.e. anything non-alcoholic, such as juice, soda, water, etc.) to a small saucepan. Sprinkle with agar-agar. Allow to soak for five minutes. Bring mixture just to a boil. Reduce to low heat, and simmer for 1 to 4 minutes (when you can see that the agar-agar is fully dissolved, it's done). Remove from heat. Working quickly, add the remaining amounts of your mixers to the agar-agar mixture and stir well. Next, stir in the liquor(s). Pour mixture into desired pan and place in refrigerator to set.

Techniques & Tips

AMONG THE MOST common questions we receive about jelly shots are 1) "Can I really make them?" and 2) "Do I need special equipment?" Rest assured that the process is quite easy, and a mind-boggling array of gorgeous jelly shots can be produced using implements no more exotic than a saucepan, a cake pan, and a sharp knife. Add a few simple decorative techniques, molds, garnishes, and a little creativity, and you can really take them a step beyond.

Our jelly shot recipes are rated from "easy" to "advanced," based on the number of steps involved. All the recipes, regardless of technique, operate largely according to the same principles: heating mixers such as juice or water over very low heat to dissolve the gelatin; stirring in liquor; and chilling until set. Recipes designated "easy" involve one cooking step (mixer plus gelatin), followed by the addition of liquors or liqueurs. A recipe such as Chai-tini could be labeled easy, apart from its reliance on incorporating homemade chai syrup (another recipe entirely); this extra—although simple—process results in an "intermediate" classification. Recipes with layers of gelatin also involve an extra step (in the form of another cooking process), and as such are labeled "intermediate," even if both layers are quite simple to make. "Advanced" recipes such as the B-52 and the Bulldog involve two or more additional steps; the B-52 has three layers, and the Bulldog includes embedded shapes.

Still wondering if you've got the goods to make jelly shots? Let's test your skill set:

* Can you operate a stove?

* Do you feel confident in your ability to use a cookie cutter? A knife? A fork?

* Are you able to set a kitchen timer, and transfer items in and out of a refrigerator based on the operation of said timer? Freezer, too?

If you answered "yes" to all of the above, you are well qualified to produce jelly shots using any of the techniques listed below. In other words, proceed with reckless abandon!

* * *

PANS

Nonreactive metal or ceramic baking pans are essential for setting jelly shots. Any size will do—loaf, mini-loaf, square, rectangular, or round. The majority of the recipes in this book yield approximately 2 cups / 480 ml gelatin mixture, and a finished jelly shot with a height of about ¾ inch / 2 cm when using a standard loaf pan. A larger pan with the same volume will produce a shorter jelly shot, while using a smaller pan for the same volume recipe will produce a jelly shot with serious stature. A recipe yielding about 2 cups / 480 ml of gelatin mixture will produce:

* 8" x 4" / 20 x 10 cm 1-pound loaf pan—about ¾-inch / 2 cm high
* Two mini loaf pans—1 cup / 240 ml volume each yields shots with a height of just under 1 inch
* 9" x 9" / 23 x 23 cm pan or 9" / 23 cm round—2 cups / 480 ml volume produces a height of about ½ inch / 2.5 cm.

As a rule, shorter jelly shots are simpler to work with—they are easier to slice, experience less "wiggle" when cutting, and are easier to remove from the pan. Taller shots are a little trickier to work with, but they deliver lots of drama at serving time.

SHAPES

Cookie cutters work best on jelly shots that are no taller than ¾ inch—anything taller wiggles around too much in the cutting process, resulting in distorted shapes. Cookie cutters in square, oval, circle, or other simple shapes work best. Complex shapes such as flowers, animals, or anything with lots of tricky angles typically warp during the cutting process, becoming unrecognizable and quite delicate to boot.

* * *

RELEASE AGENTS

Jelly shots are easy to remove from a metal or smooth ceramic pan, either by hand or with the aid of a small offset spatula. Release agents, such as oils or sprays, are not necessary unless you are using a mold. For molded shots, see instructions below.

* * *

MOLDS

Flexible silicone baking and candy molds—even silicone ice cube trays—work beautifully for making jelly shots. The advantage of using molds is that they produce a shaped shot without the scrap and waste generated when using a cookie cutter.

Molded shapes do require the use of a release agent, such as a nonstick cooking spray or a neutral-flavored vegetable oil. To prepare the mold, spray or wipe the entire mold with the oil. Next, gently wipe away all excess oil with a clean paper towel. A very fine coating of oil will be left, which will not affect the taste or appearance of the finished jelly shots, but will make it a lot easier to remove them from the molds.

angled layers

gradient layer

tinted shots

embedded shapes

When using molds, prepare the jelly shot gelatin mixture as directed, using an additional ½ envelope of gelatin to the recipe. Before filling the mold cavities, place the mold on a stable, portable surface, such as a baking sheet or cutting board. Pour or spoon the gelatin mixture into each mold cavity and transfer with the baking sheet to the refrigerator to chill until fully set. To unmold, pop the jelly shots out of the mold cavities onto your serving plate or storage container.

*   *   *

SPECIAL EFFECTS

Gelatin lends itself to a variety of beautiful and easily produced special effects.

LAYERS: Various gelatins and liqueurs can be layered, or a single jelly shot mixture can be tinted to produce a layered effect.

To make a layered shot, prepare and add the first layer of gelatin to the pan or mold and chill until fully set. Prepare the gelatin mixture for the next layer and allow it to cool slightly before carefully ladling it over the set first layer; chill until set. Continue adding layers until complete. After adding the final layer, refrigerate for several hours or overnight to allow the shot to fully set, which will prevent separation when the jelly shots are cut or unmolded.

For an angled layer in a molded shape (top left), prepare the mold as directed and place on a baking sheet. Pour the first layer of gelatin mixture into the mold and tilt the baking sheet by raising one end and resting on a small object (we find that a small yogurt or pudding container works well); chill until gelatin sets. When the first layer is set, return to level, add the final layer and chill until completely set.

GRADIENT LAYER: This technique produces layers with a fuzzy, undefined boundary. It works best for jelly shots that have two layers of varying densities, such as Tequila Sunrise, Alabama Slammer, Pom's Cup (all of which have a heavier syrup layer), and Dreamsicle (which has a heavier cream layer).

To create gradient layers, prepare the gelatin mixture for the lighter layer first, and chill in a pan or molds in the refrigerator for 10 minutes. Next, prepare the gelatin mixture for the heavier layer and allow it to cool slightly. Spoon the heavier layer into the slightly chilled first layer (it will be cool, but still liquid). The second layer will sink to the bottom, forming the gentle gradient effect. Chill until fully set.

EMBEDDED SHAPES: Prepare jelly shot gelatin mixture as directed. Tint ¼ to ½ of the gelatin mixture to desired color(s) and transfer to one or more pans (a mini loaf pan works well—the shapes should be ½ inch or less in height). Set the remaining mixture aside.

"Quick-set" the tinted mixture by placing it in the freezer for 15 to 20 minutes, until firm.

Remove from the freezer and cut the tinted set gelatin into desired shapes. Remove the shapes from the pan and transfer them to a nonstick plate or cutting board. Chill the gelatin shapes in the refrigerator for 5 to 10 minutes.

Pour the remaining untinted jelly shot mixture into desired pan. Carefully add the tinted shapes, one by one. Refrigerate until set, ideally overnight to avoid separation when the shots are cut. To serve, cut into desired shapes.

JELLY SHOTS WITH TWO DISTINCT LAYERS: Prepare the gelatin mixture for the first layer (the layer that will comprise the shapes). Pour into desired pan (a mini loaf pan works well—the shapes should

two distinct layers

eyeballs

be ½ inch or less in height) and quick-set the mixture in the freezer for 15 to 20 minutes, until firm. Transfer the pan to the refrigerator while completing the next step.

While the first layer is chilling, prepare the gelatin mixture for the second layer (the main body of the shot) and set aside.

Remove the pan containing the set first gelatin layer from the refrigerator. Using a sharp knife or cookie cutters, cut into desired shapes. Transfer the gelatin shapes to a nonstick plate or cutting board and chill in the refrigerator for 5 to 10 minutes.

Pour the reserved gelatin mixture for the main layer into desired pan.

Carefully add the chilled tinted shapes, one by one. Chill in the refrigerator until fully set, ideally overnight to avoid separation in the layers. When fully set, cut into desired shapes with a sharp knife.

EYEBALLS: Fun with either an alcohol-free recipe (see Passion Fruit Sparkler), or with a transparent jelly shot, such as Kamikaze or Gin & Tonic.

Follow the instructions for making embedded shapes, tinting ⅓ of the gelatin mixture the desired eye color (a mini loaf pan works well—keep in mind that the finished shapes should be ¼ to ½ inch in height) and quick-setting in the freezer for 15 to 20 minutes. Set the remaining gelatin mixture aside.

When the tinted gelatin is set, use a cookie cutter to cut it into small circles. Transfer the circles to a plate.

Using a small paintbrush or a cotton swab, add a dot of blue food coloring in the center of each circle to form the pupil and iris of the eyeball.

Return the shapes to the refrigerator for 15 to 20 minutes. Prepare a hemisphere mold as directed in the Molds section on page 16. Remove the plate of "eyes" from the refrigerator. Gently dab away any excess food coloring with the edge of a paper towel. Food coloring should be dry to the touch before proceeding.

Fill each of the hemisphere mold cavities with one teaspoon of the reserved untinted gelatin mixture. Place an "eye" in each mold cavity, pupil-side down. Using a teaspoon, carefully fill the cavities with the remaining gelatin mixture. Refrigerate until fully set, several hours or overnight. Unmold to serve.

BUBBLES: These are beautiful and literal in a Champagne-based jelly shot, such as the Bellini, or great for adding some textural interest, as we have done here with the Madras.

Prepare gelatin mixture per instructions (if the shot has a bottom layer, such as Bellini, prepare the bottom layer first and allow it to fully set before proceeding). Set aside half of the gelatin mixture. Pour the other half into desired pan and quick-set by placing it in the freezer for 15 to 20 minutes. Check the mixture often to avoid freezing.

When set, rake the mixture with a fork until small, uniform globules form. Distribute the raked gelatin evenly in the pan.

Pour the reserved gelatin mixture over the raked, set gelatin.

Chill until fully set, several hours or overnight.

CLOUDY DAY: An extension of the Bubbles technique above, Cloudy Day adds a great burst of color in an otherwise clear jelly shot.

Prepare gelatin mixture as directed. Set aside half of the prepared mixture, and pour the other half

into the pan specified in the recipe. Place pan in the freezer for 15 to 20 minutes to quick-set. Check often to avoid freezing.

When set, remove the gelatin mixture from the freezer. Using a fork, rake the set gelatin as described in the Bubbles technique.

Pour ⅔ of the reserved gelatin mixture over the raked gelatin. Reserve the remaining gelatin mixture.

Add a drop or two of liquid food coloring to the remaining reserved gelatin mixture. Use a teaspoon to drop spoonfuls of the tinted gelatin mixture into the pan at regular intervals.

Transfer pan to the refrigerator to chill until fully set, 2 to 3 hours. To serve, cut into desired shapes with a knife or cookie cutter.

CHECKERBOARD: This technique works well with recipes that include two distinctly colored layers of equal volume. If you have a pan with perfectly straight sides, you can make the layers on top of each other in the pan, which will save one step (see directions for Layers on page 19). Otherwise, to create a neatly aligned checkerboard pattern, prepare each layer as directed, but in separate pans. Refrigerate until very firmly set. For best results, let the layers chill overnight in the fridge.

To assemble a checkerboard jelly shot you will need: 1 cup / 240 ml water, 1 envelope gelatin, waxed paper, a small knife, and a pastry brush.

When both layers are fully set, prepare the "assembly gelatin": In a small saucepan, sprinkle the envelope of gelatin over 1 cup / 240 ml water. Allow the gelatin to soak for a minute or two. Heat over low heat, stirring constantly, until the gelatin is completely dissolved, about 5 minutes. Remove from the heat and set aside.

Remove each set gelatin layer from each pan by cutting around the edges using a sharp knife. Using your fingers, gently lift one corner of the set gelatin and gradually lift the slab from the pan, working slowly and being careful not to tear. Transfer the gelatin slabs to a clean cutting board or plate lined with waxed paper.

Using a small, sharp knife, very lightly score the top of each gelatin slab. Brush the scored surface of each gelatin slab with the assembly gelatin mixture. Place one gelatin sheet on top of the other, with scored sides facing each other. Transfer to the refrigerator to chill for 30 minutes or up to an hour. (Of course, if you have prepared the layers atop one another in one perfectly straight-sided pan, you will omit this step.)

Remove the bonded gelatin from the refrigerator and place on a clean cutting board. Using a straight-edge guide, cut the gelatin slab into slices, ½-inch / 12 mm in thickness. Lightly score one side of each slice, and brush with the assembly gelatin mixture. Flipping the slices so that alternate layers face each other, sandwich two slices together, with scored sides facing each other. Repeat with remaining gelatin slices. Chill in the refrigerator until ready to serve.

To serve, cut each piece into ½-inch / 12 mm slices.

* * *

CUTTING

Use a sharp knife with a thin profile and a long, non-serrated blade. Hold the knife perpendicular to the countertop when cutting. As is the case with hors d'oeuvres, bite-size jelly shots, or two-bite at most, are easiest to handle—no more than 1 to 1½ square inches (2.5 to 4 cm) of jelly shot.

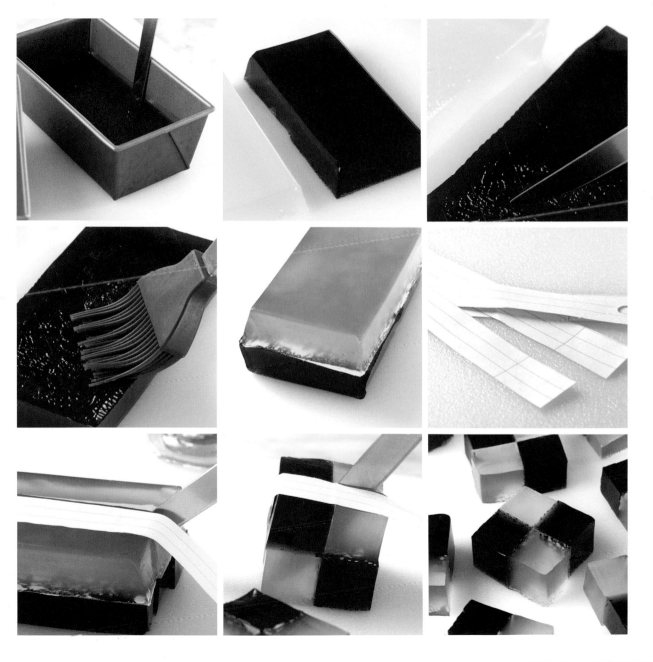

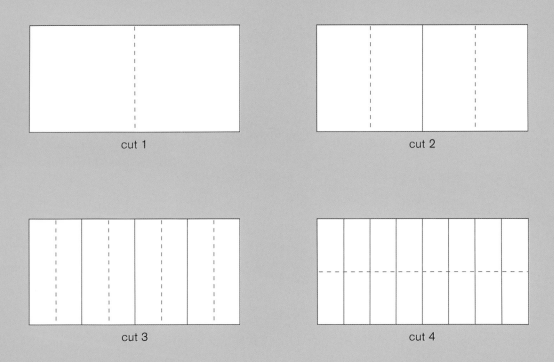

cut 1

cut 2

cut 3

cut 4

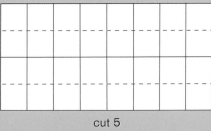

cut 5

The easiest way to slice uniform shots is to use a paper guide when cutting. Cut out desired widths from graph paper, then place (don't press) on top of the set gelatin mixture, using the paper as a knife guide.

Another easy method is to make a series of cuts, dividing the set gelatin first into two parts, then dividing each part again in two, working from vertical to horizontal cuts until the shots are the desired size. The diagram on the facing page illustrates step-by-step cuts (in red) for a standard loaf pan, yielding 32 jelly shots.

* * *

GARNISH

Our favorite garnishes are traditional ones, in that they are usually small slivers of the garnish you might find served with a given jelly shot's cocktail inspiration. Traditional garnishes are also functional: they can assist with identification of the jelly shots, enabling guests to easily distinguish, say, a Tom Collins jelly shot from a Gimlet.

Traditional garnishes can run the gamut from full-on "fruit salads" to simple and elegant citrus zests, slivered or chopped.

Other jelly shot garnish options include flavored sugars, large-crystal sugar, chocolate shavings, or cookie crumbs for dipping. With fragile garnishes such as these, garnish and serve the jelly shots in small batches that will be consumed immediately, as the water in the gelatin will rapidly deteriorate the garnish. Another option: Set out a small bowl of the garnish with a plate of nude jelly shots for self-serve dipping as a fun alternative.

garnish

skewers

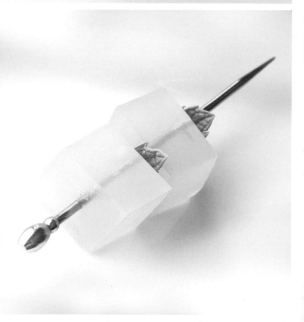

* * *

SERVING

MAKE AHEAD – YES OR NO?

While Jelly Shots can certainly be made a day in advance, we don't recommend cutting and plating until very near serving time as the delicate taste profile of the jelly shot appears to dissipate once cut. For best results, prepare jelly shots the night before or morning of your event. The jelly shots may be cut an hour or so ahead, and stored on a nonstick cookie sheet in the refrigerator until they can be plated for serving.

CHALLENGING CLIMATE CONDITIONS
(I.E HEAT AND HUMIDITY)

Jelly shots are a hit at warm-weather gatherings! As such, we wanted to share a few tips to help your jelly shots pass muster under challenging conditions:

* When serving jelly shots al fresco, you may wish to add an extra ½ envelope of gelatin to the recipe. The texture won't be quite as tender, but it will give your jelly shots a little extra oomph on a hot day.
* Chill your serving platter before plating the jelly shots.
* Plate only as many jelly shots as will be consumed immediately. (A plus: This also adds drama when you return to the party every so often bearing new and exciting varieties!)

SKEWERING

Jelly shots are adorable threaded onto tiny cocktail skewers. When serving shots this way, we add an extra ½ envelope of gelatin to the recipe to give the shots more firmness and stability.

Groupings & Flights

FOR EASY ENTERTAINING, we have included the following suggestions for jelly shot groupings. The groupings are by no means comprehensive, rather they offer a medley of jelly shots to fulfill a specific theme, and are tied together by a base flavor or otherwise combine well for a mixed platter. Jelly shot flights, on the other hand, are sets of three or four jelly shots which progress like traditional wine or Champagne tastings: from airy to bold and light to dark. Or they simply flit between spirits with a smooth transition. Have fun with your own spirited and inspired combinations!

* * *

GROUPINGS

PATIO

Cosmopolitan

Piña Colada

Mai Tai

Fuzzy Navel

Sea Breeze

Madras

BRUNCH-TASTIC

Pimm's Cup

Bellini

Melon Ball

Bee's Knees

Champagne Cocktail

Champagne & Liqueur

Blood Orange Screwdriver

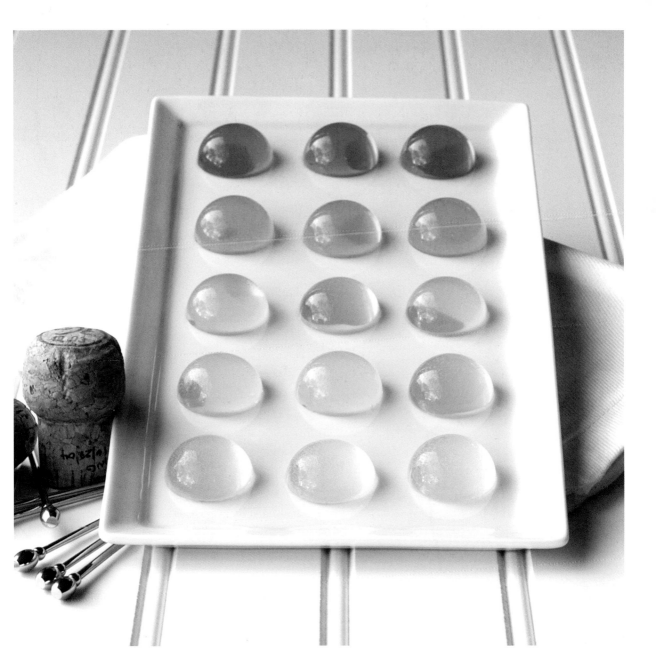

tropical grouping

FLASHBACK FAVORITES

Tom Collins

Lemon Drop

Kamikaze

Raspberry Kamikaze

Long Island Iced Tea

CLASSIC/RETRO

Sidecar

Gin & Juice

Manhattan

Old Fashioned

Mint Julep

Jack Rose

Negroni

Aviation

French 75

TROPICAL

Blue

Mai Tai

Oasis Breeze

Banana Daiquiri

Strawberry Daiquiri

Piña Colada

DESSERT

Grasshopper

B-52

Peanut Butter & Jelly Martini

White Chocolate Martini

Baileys & Coffee

Sambuca

Key Lime Pie Martini

SEASONAL – SPRING & SUMMER

Bellini

Vodka Pink Lemonade

Mojito

Caipirinha

Key Lime Martini

Tequila Sunrise

SEASONAL – FALL & WINTER

Apple Martini

Kir Royale

Blood Orange Screwdriver

Pomegranate Martini

Chai-tini

* * *

FLIGHTS

AGE OF FLIGHT
BASE FLAVOR: Transition from Crème
de Violette to Lemon

Champagne & Liqueur
(with crème de violette)

Aviation

Lemon Drop

Lynchburg Lemonade

LIME TIME
BASE FLAVOR: Lime

Cucumber-Lime Saketini

Mojito

Caipirinha

Gimlet

BIG APPLE
BASE FLAVOR: Apple

Apple Martini

Jack Rose

Washington Apple

BUBBLES ARE
A GIRL'S BEST FRIEND
BASE SPIRIT: Champagne

Kir Royale

Flirtini

French 75

DON'T FORGET TO PACK THE GIN
BASE SPIRIT: Gin

Gin & Tonic

Tom Collins

Gin & Juice

BITTERS ARE THE NEW BLACK
BASE FLAVOR: Bitters

Champagne Cocktail

Old Fashioned

Manhattan

Negroni

bitters are the new black

pretty in pink

PARISIAN FLING

BASE FLAVOR: Lemon

Bee's Knees

Lemon Meringue

French 75

Sidecar

SOUTH OF THE MASON-DIXON

BASE SPIRIT: Whiskey

Mint Julep

Lynchburg Lemonade

Hurricane

Alabama Slammer

PRETTY IN PINK

BASE SPIRIT: Vodka

Vodka Pink Lemonade

Raspberry Kamikaze

Sea Breeze

Cosmopolitan

NO TEA FOR ME

BASE FLAVOR: Coffee

Mudslide

White Russian

Baileys & Coffee

B-52

FOR THE GENTLEMEN'S LOUNGE

BASE ATTRIBUTE: Masculinity

Arnie Palmer

Long Island Iced Tea

Old Fashioned

Manhattan

The Jelly Shot
Recipes

Alabama Slammer

Difficulty: Intermediate

Recommended Pan: 1–pound loaf pan
(approximately 8" x 4" / 20 x 10 cm)

Orange Layer

¾ cup / 180 ml orange juice

1½ envelopes Knox gelatin

¼ cup / 60 ml Southern Comfort

¼ cup / 60 ml vodka

¼ cup / 60 ml sloe gin

Grenadine Layer

½ cup / 120 ml Pomegranate Syrup
(see recipe on page 198)

½ envelope Knox gelatin

Hawaiian Punch for grown-ups! Our version of the Alabama Slammer is made with homemade pomegranate syrup (see the Syrup Recipes section beginning on page 195). Rose's grenadine syrup or another purchased grenadine syrup will also work, but will lack the vibrant purple color (and tangy pomegranate taste) of the homemade version. We used the Gradient Layer method to make the jellies; see the Techniques section (page 14) for full details.

ORANGE LAYER Pour orange juice into a small saucepan and sprinkle with the 1½ envelope portion of gelatin. Allow the gelatin to soak for a minute or two. Heat over very low heat until gelatin is dissolved, stirring constantly, about 5 minutes. Stir in the Southern Comfort, vodka, and sloe gin. Pour mixture into loaf pan. Place in refrigerator to cool while preparing Grenadine Layer.

GRENADINE LAYER Pour the Pomegranate Syrup into a small saucepan and sprinkle with the ½ envelope of gelatin; allow to soak for a minute or two. Heat over very low heat until gelatin is dissolved, stirring constantly, about 4 minutes. Remove from the heat and transfer to a bowl. Remove the orange juice mixture from the refrigerator (mixture will still be liquid). Drop spoonfuls of the grenadine mixture at regular intervals into the orange mixture. Repeat until all the grenadine mixture has been used. Do not stir. Carefully return pan to refrigerator and chill until fully set, several hours or overnight.

To serve, cut into desired shapes. Makes 18 to 24 jelly shots.

Apple Martini,
Sour and Sweet

Difficulty: Easy

Recommended Pan: Molds or two mini loaf pans (approximately 6" × 3" / 15 × 7.5 cm)

⅔ cup / 165 ml apple juice

2 envelopes Knox gelatin

⅓ cup / 75 ml Apfelkorn
(or other sweet apple liqueur)

⅓ cup / 75 ml De Kuyper Sour Apple
Pucker schnapps

⅔ cup / 165 ml vodka, divided

Mellow yet tart, Sour and Sweet Apple Martini jelly shots are a perfect choice for holiday gatherings. We love to separate the sweet and sour apple liqueurs and make two smaller batches, either using silicon molds or two mini loaf pans. The resulting pale yellow and pale green shots look beautiful plated together, and provide a variety of taste.

POUR APPLE JUICE into a small saucepan and sprinkle with the gelatin. Allow the gelatin to soak for a minute or two. Heat over very low heat, stirring constantly, until gelatin is dissolved, about 5 minutes. Divide the mixture equally between two separate bowls. Add the Apfelkorn to one portion, and the Apple Pucker to the other. Stir each well to blend. Pour into pans or molds and chill until fully set, several hours or overnight.

To serve, cut into desired shapes. Makes 16 to 24 jelly shots.

Arnie Palmer
(3-Sheets Version)

Difficulty: Intermediate
Recommended Pan: 1–pound loaf pan
(approximately 8" × 4" / 20 × 10 cm)

Tea Layer

½ cup / 120 ml brewed
  unsweetened black tea

1 envelope Knox gelatin

½ cup / 120 ml sweet tea vodka

1 to 2 teaspoons Simple Syrup
  (see recipe on page 198)
  or agave nectar, if desired

Lemonade Layer

⅔ cup / 165 ml Lemon Syrup
  (see recipe on page 197)

1 envelope Knox gelatin

⅓ cup / 75 ml vodka

Our vodka-spiked version of the teetotaler's warm-weather staple, Arnie Palmer jelly shots are refreshing on a summer's day. Bottled, unsweetened iced tea may be substituted for the brewed tea called for in the recipe. If you brew your own tea, adhere to the directions as oversteeping can result in a pronounced bitter flavor.

TEA LAYER Pour the brewed tea into a small saucepan and sprinkle with the gelatin. Allow the gelatin to soak for a minute or two. Heat the mixture over very low heat, stirring constantly, until gelatin is dissolved, about 5 minutes. Remove from the heat and stir in the sweet tea vodka. Taste and add the simple syrup, if desired. Pour mixture into loaf pan and refrigerate until set, 1 to 2 hours. (When set, the mixture will be cloudy.) Prepare the Lemonade Layer.

LEMONADE LAYER Pour the lemon syrup into a small saucepan and sprinkle with the gelatin. Allow the gelatin to soak for a minute or two. Heat the mixture over very low heat, stirring constantly, until gelatin is dissolved, about 5 minutes. Remove from the heat, and stir in the vodka. Allow the mixture to cool slightly.

Remove the set Tea Layer from the refrigerator. Using a fork, rake the set mixture until small, uniform globules form. Ladle the Lemonade mixture into the pan over the Tea Layer. Return the pan to the refrigerator until fully set, several hours or overnight.

To serve, cut into desired shapes. Makes 18 to 24 jelly shots.

Aviation

Difficulty: Easy
Recommended Pan: 1–pound loaf pan
(approximately 8" x 4" / 20 x 10 cm)

⅔ cup / 165 ml Lemon Syrup
  (see recipe on page 197)
⅔ cup / 165 ml water
2 envelopes Knox gelatin
⅔ cup / 165 ml Hendrick's gin
1 tablespoon maraschino liqueur
  (clear variety, not red)
2 tablespoons crème de violette
Lemon zest for garnish, if desired

The Aviation is a classic gin-based cocktail popular in the 1920s. Its subtle, steely grey color comes courtesy of the crème de violette liqueur. The subtle flavors of a new-style gin, such as Hendrick's, are a must for this jelly shot.

COMBINE THE LEMON syrup and water in a small saucepan and sprinkle with the gelatin. Allow the gelatin to soak for a minute or two. Heat over very low heat until gelatin is dissolved, stirring constantly, about 5 minutes. Stir in the gin and both liqueurs. Transfer the mixture to loaf pan. Refrigerate until fully set several hours or overnight.

To serve, cut into desired shapes. Garnish with lemon zest, if desired. Makes 18 to 24 jelly shots.

B-52

Difficulty: Advanced
Recommended Pan: 1–pound loaf pan
(approximately 8" x 4" / 20 x 10 cm)

Kahlúa Layer
½ cup / 120 ml brewed coffee
   or espresso
1 envelope Knox gelatin
½ cup / 120 ml Kahlúa coffee liqueur

Grand Marnier Layer
1 cup / 240 ml Grand Marnier
1 envelope Knox gelatin

Baileys Layer
½ cup / 120 ml water
1 envelope Knox gelatin
½ cup / 120 ml Baileys Irish
   cream liqueur

N ot just for Rock Lobsters and dropping conventional muni-tions in combat, B-52 jelly shots always make a dramatic entrance. Serve in very small cubes or thin slices.

KAHLÚA LAYER Pour the coffee into a small saucepan and sprin-kle with the gelatin. Allow the gelatin to soak for a minute or two. Heat over very low heat, stirring constantly, until gelatin is fully dis-solved, about 5 minutes. Remove from the heat and stir in the Kahlúa. Pour mixture into loaf pan. Chill until fully set, at least one hour. Prepare Grand Marnier Layer.

GRAND MARNIER LAYER Pour in the Grand Marnier into a small saucepan and sprinkle with the gelatin. Allow the gelatin to soak for a minute or two. Heat over very low heat, stirring constantly, until gelatin is fully dissolved, about 5 minutes. (Take care to use very low heat, to avoid overheating the alcohol.) Remove from the heat and allow to cool slightly. Remove the chilled Kahlúa layer from the refrigerator and carefully spoon the Grand Marnier mixture over the top. Return to the refrigerator and chill until fully set, at least one hour. Prepare Baileys Layer.

BAILEYS LAYER Pour the water into a small saucepan and sprinkle with the gelatin. Allow the gelatin to soak for a minute or two. Heat over very low heat, stirring constantly, until gelatin is fully dissolved, about 5 minutes. Remove from the heat and stir in the Irish cream. Allow the mixture to cool slightly before carefully ladling over the chilled Grand Marnier layer. Chill until fully set, ideally overnight.

To serve, cut into small squares or rectangles. Makes 24 to 36 small jelly shots.

Baileys & Coffee

Difficulty: Intermediate
Recommended Pan: 9" × 9" / 23 × 23 cm square or 9" / 23 cm round

Coffee Layer

1 cup / 240 ml brewed dark roast coffee or espresso
2 envelopes Knox gelatin
1 cup / 240 ml Kahlúa coffee liqueur

Baileys Layer

½ cup / 120 ml water
2 envelopes Knox gelatin
1½ cups / 360 ml Baileys Irish cream liqueur

B aileys and Coffee jelly shots are always crowd pleasers. Perfect for an after-dinner treat or by the fire.

COFFEE LAYER Pour brewed coffee into a medium saucepan and sprinkle with gelatin. Allow the gelatin to soak for a minute or two. Heat over very low heat, stirring constantly, until gelatin is fully dissolved, about 5 minutes. Remove from the heat and add the Kahlúa, stirring well to blend. Pour mixture into pan. Refrigerate until set, at least 1 hour. Prepare Baileys Layer.

BAILEYS LAYER Pour the water into a medium saucepan and sprinkle with the gelatin. Allow the gelatin to soak for a minute or two. Heat over low heat until gelatin is fully dissolved, about 5 minutes. (Mixture will initially be very thick.) Remove from the heat and strain through a fine mesh strainer to remove any remaining gelatin solids. Stir the Baileys into the strained mixture, mixing carefully and thoroughly to blend the liqueur. Allow to cool slightly.

Remove the chilled Coffee Layer from refrigerator. Carefully ladle the Baileys Layer onto the chilled Coffee Layer. Return pan to refrigerator and chill until fully set, several hours or overnight.

To serve, cut into desired shapes. Makes 18 to 24 jelly shots.

Bee's Knees

Difficulty: Easy
Recommended Pan: 1-pound loaf pan
(approximately 8" x 4" / 20 x 10 cm)

⅔ cup / 165 ml Lemon Syrup
   (see recipe on page 197)
⅓ cup / 75 ml honey
⅓ cup / 75 ml water
2 envelopes Knox gelatin
⅔ cup / 165 ml gin

J ust thinking about these honey-flavored, gin-based jelly shots makes us want to head out to the gazebo. That is, if we had a gazebo. We might just build one, expressly to enjoy a plate of these brunch-tastic little beauties out among the flora and fauna once in a while.

COMBINE THE LEMON syrup, honey, and water in a medium saucepan and sprinkle with gelatin. Allow the gelatin to soak for a minute or two. Heat over low heat, stirring constantly, until gelatin is fully dissolved, about 5 minutes. Remove from the heat and stir in the gin. Pour the mixture into loaf pan and chill until fully set, several hours or overnight.

To serve, cut into desired shapes. Makes 18 to 24 jelly shots.

Bellini

Difficulty: Intermediate
Recommended Pan: 9" × 9" / 23 × 23 cm or
9" / 23 cm round

Peach Layer

½ cup / 120 ml peach juice or peach
   nectar (strained through a fine sieve
   to remove solids)
1 envelope Knox gelatin
½ cup / 120 ml peach schnapps

Prosecco Layer

1½ cups / 360 ml Prosecco,
   Champagne, or other white
   sparkling wine
½ cup / 120 ml water
2 tablespoons granulated sugar
2 envelopes Knox gelatin
Thin slivers of fresh or canned
   peach and mint leaves for garnish,
   if desired

The Bellini jelly shot is adorable cut into rounds and garnished with a thin sliver of peach and a mint sprig. For best results, make these the day you plan to serve them, and cut them out as soon as they are fully set to ensure a clean cut with minimal distortion. Try a variation on the Bellini by replacing the peach nectar with another juice or purée, such as raspberry or blueberry.

PEACH LAYER Pour the peach juice into a medium saucepan and sprinkle with the gelatin. Allow the gelatin to soak for a minute or two. Heat over low heat, stirring constantly, until gelatin is fully dissolved, about 5 minutes. Remove from the heat and stir in the schnapps. Pour the mixture into a pan and refrigerate until fully set (about an hour) before preparing the Prosecco Layer.

PROSECCO LAYER Combine the Prosecco, water, and sugar in a medium sauce-pan and sprinkle with the gelatin. Allow the gelatin to soak for a minute or two. Heat over very low heat, stirring constantly, until gelatin is dissolved, about 5 minutes. (Take care to use very low heat to avoid overheating the alcohol.) The mixture will initially be foamy, but the foam will diminish. Strain to remove any gelatin solids. Allow to cool slightly.

Ladle the Prosecco mixture over the set Peach Layer. Return to the refrigerator and chill until fully set, several hours or overnight.

To serve, cut into desired shapes. Garnish each jelly shot with a thin sliver of peach and mint, if desired. Makes 24 to 30 jelly shots.

Black Russian

Difficulty: Easy
Recommended Pan: 1–pound loaf pan
(approximately 8" x 4" / 20 x 10 cm)

⅔ cup / 165 ml brewed strong coffee
  or espresso
2 envelopes Knox gelatin
⅔ cup / 165 ml Kahlúa coffee liqueur
⅔ cup / 165 ml vodka

Created in honor of the U.S. ambassador to Luxembourg in 1949, the Black Russian was perhaps the first popular coffee cocktail. The "Russian" was a nod to the use of vodka, a relative newcomer to the American cocktail scene at the time. Like its liquid inspiration, the Black Russian jelly shot is the ideal blend of sharp and sweet—and is a perfect after-dinner treat.

POUR THE COFFEE into a medium saucepan and sprinkle with the gelatin. Allow the gelatin to soak for a minute or two. Heat over very low heat until gelatin is dissolved, stirring constantly, about 5 minutes. Remove from the heat and stir in the Kahlúa and vodka. Pour the mixture into loaf pan. Refrigerate until fully set, several hours or overnight.

To serve, cut into desired shapes. Makes 18 to 24 jelly shots.

Blue Hawaii

Difficulty: Intermediate
Recommended Pan: 1–pound loaf pan (approximately 8" x 4" / 20 x 10 cm) or molds

Blue Layer

¼ cup / 60 ml pineapple juice, strained to remove solids

¼ cup / 60 ml vodka

1 envelope Knox gelatin

¼ cup / 60 ml blue curaçao liqueur

¼ cup / 60 ml white rum

Yellow Layer

¾ cup / 180 ml pineapple juice, strained to remove solids

¼ cup / 60 ml Lemon Syrup (see recipe on page 197)

1 envelope Knox gelatin

A classic tiki drink, the Blue Hawaii cocktail gets its distinctive tropical tint from blue curaçao liqueur. It differs from the Blue Hawaiian, a blended drink that includes Coco Lopez cream of coconut. If you are coconut fan, try substituting Malibu coconut rum for the white rum used in the blue layer.

BLUE LAYER Combine the pineapple juice and vodka in a small saucepan and sprinkle with the gelatin. Allow the gelatin to soak for a minute or two. Heat over low heat, stirring constantly, until gelatin is fully dissolved, about 5 minutes. (Take care to use very low heat, to avoid overheating the alcohol.) Remove from the heat and stir in the curaçao and rum. Transfer mixture to loaf pan or molds and refrigerate for at least an hour or until fully set. Prepare Yellow Layer.

YELLOW LAYER Combine the pineapple juice and lemon syrup in a small saucepan and sprinkle with the gelatin. Allow the gelatin to soak for a minute or two. Heat over very low heat, stirring constantly, until gelatin is dissolved, about 5 minutes. Remove from the heat and allow to cool slightly. Remove set Blue Layer from refrigerator, and ladle the yellow gelatin mixture over the top. Refrigerate until fully set, several hours or overnight.

To serve, cut into desired shapes or unmold shots. Makes 18 to 24 jelly shots.

Caipirinha

Difficulty: Intermediate
Recommended Pan: 1–pound loaf pan
(approximately 8" x 4" / 20 x 10 cm)

1½ cups / 360 ml Lime Syrup
(see recipe on page 197)

2½ envelopes Knox gelatin

1 cup / 240 ml cachaça

2 teaspoons finely chopped lime zest

Additional 1½ teaspoons finely
chopped lime zest for garnish,
if desired

The national cocktail of Brazil, the Caipirinha is a bold combination of cachaça, a sugar cane-based brandy, limes, and just enough sugar to take the edge off. The name itself is a diminutive of the Brazilian word for "countryman." This jelly shot could be made with rum in a pinch, but we highly recommend the cachaça version.

POUR THE LIME syrup into a medium saucepan and sprinkle with the gelatin. Allow the gelatin to soak for a minute or two. Heat over low heat, stirring constantly, until gelatin is dissolved, about 5 minutes. Remove from the heat and stir in the cachaça and lime zest. Pour the mixture into loaf pan and chill until set, several hours or overnight.

To serve, cut into desired shapes. Garnish with finely chopped lime zest, if desired. Makes 18 to 24 jelly shots.

Chai-tini

Difficulty: Intermediate
Recommended Pan: 1–pound loaf pan
(approximately 8" x 4" / 20 x 10 cm)
or molds

½ cup / 120 ml Chai Syrup
  (see recipe on page 196)
½ cup / 120 ml milk (whole or 2%)
2 envelopes Knox gelatin
¼ cup / 60 ml Baileys caramel liqueur
1 cup / 240 ml ginger-flavored vodka
Cinnamon sugar for garnish,
  if desired

Sweet and spicy, the Chai-tini jelly shot is wonderful on its own or as an accompaniment to other dessert jelly shots.

COMBINE THE CHAI syrup and milk in a medium saucepan and sprinkle with the gelatin. Allow the gelatin to soak for a minute or two. Heat over low heat until gelatin is dissolved, stirring constantly, about 5 minutes. (Mixture will be quite thick initially.) Remove from the heat and stir in the Baileys, and then the vodka. Strain mixture to remove any gelatin solids. Pour the strained mixture into loaf pan or molds. Refrigerate until fully set, several hours or overnight.

To serve, cut into desired shapes or unmold shots. Immediately before serving, dip one edge of each jelly shot into cinnamon sugar, or serve with a small bowl of cinnamon sugar to allow guests to garnish their own, if desired. (No double dipping!) Makes 18 to 24 jelly shots.

Champagne & Liqueur

Difficulty: Easy
Recommended Pan: 9" × 9" / 23 × 23 cm
square or 9" / 23 cm round

1½ cups / 360 ml Champagne,
   Prosecco, or other white
   sparkling wine
½ cup / 120 ml water
2 tablespoons granulated sugar
2 envelopes Knox gelatin
2 tablespoons liqueur or cordial (add
   after heating)
Edible flowers for garnish, if desired

Champagne combines beautifully with an array of liqueurs, such as crème de violette, green Chartreuse, St. Germain, Chambord, or Cointreau to make a delicate, elegantly flavored jelly shot. Try a mixed plate of Champagne & Liqueur jelly shots as a lovely, pastel-toned accompaniment to a cheese course.

COMBINE CHAMPAGNE, water, and sugar in a medium saucepan and sprinkle with the gelatin. Allow the gelatin to soak for a minute or two. Heat over very low heat, stirring constantly, until gelatin is dissolved, about 5 minutes. (Take care to use very low heat to avoid overheating alcohol.) Mixture will initially be foamy, but this will diminish. Remove from the heat and strain the mixture to remove any remaining gelatin solids. Stir the liqueur into the strained mixture and pour into pan. Refrigerate until fully set, several hours or overnight.

To serve, cut into shapes. Garnish with edible flower petals, if desired. Makes 18 to 24 jelly shots.

Champagne Cocktail

Difficulty: Intermediate
Recommended Pan: 9" × 9" / 23 × 23 cm
square or 9" / 23 cm round

Bitters Layer
½ cup / 120 ml Bitters Syrup
  (see recipe on page 196)
½ envelope Knox gelatin

Champagne Layer
1½ cups / 360 ml Champagne,
  Prosecco, or other white
  sparkling wine
½ cup / 120 ml water
1 tablespoon granulated sugar
2 envelopes Knox gelatin

Just like its delightful namesake aperitif, the Champagne Cocktail jelly shot is a welcome and festive addition to any gathering. These are equally delicious when made with Prosecco, Cava, or your favorite sparkling wine in place of Champagne.

BITTERS LAYER Pour the Bitters syrup into a small saucepan and sprinkle with the gelatin. Allow the gelatin to soak for a minute or two. Heat over low heat, stirring constantly, until gelatin is dissolved, about 5 minutes. Pour mixture into pan, and chill until fully set, at least an hour. Prepare Champagne Layer.

CHAMPAGNE LAYER Combine the Champagne, water, and sugar in a medium saucepan and sprinkle with the gelatin. Allow the gelatin to soak for a minute or two. Heat over very low heat, stirring constantly, until gelatin is dissolved, about 5 minutes. Mixture will initially be very foamy; however, this will diminish. (Take care to heat over very low heat to avoid overheating alcohol.) Strain mixture to remove any remaining gelatin solids. Allow the strained mixture to cool slightly, then pour over the set Bitters Layer. Return the pan to the refrigerator and allow to set fully, several hours or overnight.

To serve, cut into desired shapes. Makes 24 to 32 jelly shots.

Chocolate Martini

Difficulty: Intermediate
Recommended Pan: 1–pound loaf pan
(approximately 8" x 4" / 20 x 10 cm)

"Ganache" Layer

½ cup / 120 ml chocolate milk

1 envelope Knox gelatin

½ cup / 120 ml Godiva dark
   chocolate liqueur

Martini Layer

½ cup / 120 ml milk (whole or 2%)

2 envelopes Knox gelatin

½ cup / 120 ml Godiva dark
   chocolate liqueur

½ cup / 120 ml vanilla-flavored vodka

¼ cup / 60 ml Baileys Irish
   cream liqueur

Chocolate shavings for garnish

We love the contrast of the chocolate ganache layer with the chocolate Martini layer. Serve these solo or with other dessert jelly shot options, such as White Chocolate Martini or Chai-tini.

"GANACHE" LAYER Pour the chocolate milk into a small saucepan and sprinkle with the gelatin. Allow the gelatin to soak for a minute or two. Heat mixture over low heat until gelatin is fully dissolved, stirring constantly, about 5 minutes. Remove from the heat and allow to cool slightly. Stir in chocolate liqueur. Pour mixture into loaf pan and chill until fully set, one to two hours. Prepare Martini Layer.

MARTINI LAYER Pour the milk into a medium saucepan and sprinkle with the gelatin. Allow the gelatin to soak for a minute or two. Heat over low heat, stirring constantly, until gelatin is fully dissolved about 5 minutes. Remove from the heat and allow to cool slightly. Stir in the chocolate liqueur, vodka, and the Baileys.

Remove the chilled ganache layer from the refrigerator. Pour the martini mixture gently over the top. Return the pan to the refrigerator and chill until fully set, one to two hours.

To serve, cut into desired shapes. Garnish with chocolate shavings, if desired. Makes 18 to 24 jelly shots.

Colorado Bulldog

Difficulty: Advanced
Recommended Pan: 1–pound loaf pan
(approximately 8" x 4" / 20 x 10 cm)

Kahlúa-Vodka Layer
½ cup / 120 ml milk (whole or 2%)
1½ envelopes Knox gelatin
½ cup / 120 ml Kahlúa coffee liqueur
½ cup / 120 ml vodka

Cola Layer
½ cup / 120 ml cola
½ envelope Knox gelatin

This jelly shot is beautiful prepared as shown, using the Embedded Shapes technique with the cola layer comprising the "dots" (see Techniques section for details). It can also be prepared as a simple layered shot, as described below.

KAHLÚA-VODKA LAYER Pour the milk into a small saucepan and sprinkle with the gelatin. Allow the gelatin to soak for a minute or two. Heat over very low heat until gelatin is dissolved, stirring constantly, about 5 minutes. Remove from the heat and stir in the Kahlúa, and then the vodka. Pour mixture into loaf pan and refrigerate until fully set, at least an hour. Prepare Cola Layer.

COLA LAYER Pour the cola into a small saucepan and sprinkle with the gelatin. Allow the gelatin to soak for a minute or two. Heat over very low heat until gelatin is dissolved, stirring constantly, about 5 minutes. Remove from the heat and allow to cool slightly. Pour cola mixture over set Kahlúa-Vodka Layer and refrigerate until fully set, several hours or overnight.

To serve, cut into desired shapes. Makes 18 to 24 jelly shots.

Cosmopolitan

Difficulty: Easy

Recommended Pan: 1–pound loaf pan (approximately 8" x 4" / 20 x 10 cm)

- 1 cup / 240 ml cranberry juice cocktail
- ¼ cup / 60 ml Lime Syrup (see recipe on page 197) or Rose's lime juice
- 2 envelopes Knox gelatin
- ¾ cup / 180 ml orange-flavored vodka
- ¼ cup / 60 ml Grand Marnier
- Lime zest for garnish, if desired

This pink cocktail was notably quaffed by the character Carrie Bradshaw on the HBO series *Sex and the City* in the late 1990s. Temporarily overexposed for a time, the Cosmopolitan remains a delight to the palate and is just as crisp and refreshing in gelatin form.

COMBINE THE CRANBERRY juice cocktail and lime syrup in a medium saucepan and sprinkle with the gelatin. Allow the gelatin to soak for a few minutes. Heat on low, stirring constantly, until gelatin is fully dissolved, about 5 minutes. Remove from the heat and stir in the vodka and Grand Marnier, stirring well to blend. Pour mixture into loaf pan and chill until fully set, several hours or overnight.

To serve, cut into desired shapes. Garnish with the lime zest, if desired. Makes 18 to 24 jelly shots.

Cuba Libre

Difficulty: Easy
Recommended Pan: 1–pound loaf pan
(approximately 8" x 4" / 20 x 10 cm)

1⅓ cups / 315 ml cola
2 envelopes Knox gelatin
⅔ cup / 165 ml rum
1 tablespoon Rose's lime juice
Lime zest for garnish, if desired

This favorite cocktail of freedom fighters everywhere is otherwise known as the standard bar favorite, the Rum and Coke (with lime, please).

POUR THE COLA into a medium saucepan and sprinkle with the gelatin. Allow the gelatin to soak for a minute or two. Heat over very low heat until gelatin is dissolved, stirring constantly, about 5 minutes. Remove from the heat and stir in the rum and the Rose's lime juice. Pour mixture into loaf pan and refrigerate until fully set, several hours or overnight.

To serve, cut into desired shapes. Garnish with lime zest, if desired. Makes 18 to 24 jelly shots.

Cucumber–Lime Saketini

Difficulty: Easy
Recommended Pan: 1–pound loaf pan (approximately 8" x 4" / 20 x 10 cm)
Implements: Cocktail shaker and cocktail muddler

1 (1-inch / 2.5 cm) piece cucumber, coarsely chopped

⅔ cup / 165 ml sake

6 ice cubes

⅔ cup / 165 ml Lime Syrup (see recipe on page 197)

2 envelopes Knox gelatin

⅔ cup / 165 ml vodka

1 teaspoon agave nectar

There are several versions of the cocktail inspiration for this jelly shot. Some use vodka, some use gin, and others add flavor with a liqueur, such as orange curaçao. Our version contains vodka, and is flavored with cucumber and lime. A new-style gin, such as Hendrick's, is also very nice in these.

IN A COCKTAIL shaker, muddle the cucumber. Add the sake and ice cubes to the shaker and shake vigorously. Strain the liquid into a glass and set aside. You should have ⅔ cup / 165 ml liquid.

Pour the lime syrup into a medium saucepan and sprinkle with the gelatin. Allow the gelatin to soak for a few minutes. Heat carefully over very low heat until gelatin is fully dissolved, approximately 5 minutes. Remove from the heat and stir in the vodka, reserved cucumber-sake liquid, and the agave nectar. Pour mixture into loaf pan and refrigerate until fully set, several hours or overnight.

To serve, cut into desired shapes. Makes 18 to 24 jelly shots.

Daiquiri, Banana

Difficulty: Intermediate
Recommended Pan: 1–pound loaf pan
(approximately 8" × 4" / 20 × 10 cm)

¾ cup / 180 ml Lime Syrup
  (see recipe on page 197) or
  Rose's lime juice

2 envelopes Knox gelatin

1 cup / 240 ml white rum

¾ cup / 180 ml banana liqueur

Bananas and lemon juice for garnish,
  if desired

Serve our interpretation of the potent frozen cocktail delight on thin slices of banana to add fresh fruit flavor. Brushing the banana slices with a little lemon juice will prevent browning. These are beautiful served solo, or on a mixed plate with Strawberry Daiquiri jelly shots.

POUR THE LIME syrup into a medium saucepan and sprinkle with the gelatin. Allow the gelatin to soak for a minute or two. Heat over low heat, stirring constantly, until gelatin is dissolved, about 5 minutes. Remove from the heat and stir in the rum and banana liqueur. Pour mixture into loaf pan and refrigerate until fully set, several hours or overnight.

To serve, cut into desired shapes. Cut banana into ¼-inch / 6 mm slices, if using. If desired, lightly brush each banana slice with lemon juice to prevent browning. Dab each banana slice very lightly with a paper towel. Place each jelly shot on a banana slice. Makes 18 to 24 jelly shots.

Daiquiri, Strawberry

Difficulty: Intermediate
Recommended Pan: 1–pound loaf pan
(approximately 8" x 4" / 20 x 10 cm)

½ cup / 120 ml Lime Syrup
(see recipe on page 197) or
Rose's lime juice

6 tablespoons Strawberry Syrup
(see recipe on page 198) or
purchased strawberry syrup,
such as Monin brand

4 teaspoons granulated sugar

2 envelopes Knox gelatin

1 cup / 240 ml white rum

¼ cup / 60 ml strawberry schnapps
or strawberry liqueur

Strawberries for garnish, if desired

Papa Hemingway probably wouldn't approve, but who else doesn't love a strawberry daiquiri? We serve each jelly shot on a strawberry slice for an extra punch of fresh fruit flavor. These are delicious served on their own, or on a mixed plate with Banana Daiquiri jelly shots or other tropical favorites.

COMBINE THE LIME syrup, strawberry syrup, and sugar in a small saucepan and sprinkle with the gelatin. Allow the gelatin to soak for a few minutes. Heat over low heat, stirring constantly, until gelatin is dissolved, about 5 minutes. Remove from the heat and stir in the rum and strawberry schnapps. Pour mixture into loaf pan and refrigerate until set, several hours or overnight.

To serve, cut into desired shapes. Cut strawberries into ¼-inch / 6 mm slices, if using. Place each jelly shot on a strawberry slice. Makes 18 to 24 jelly shots.

Dreamsicle

Difficulty: Advanced

Recommended Pan: 1–pound loaf pan (approximately 8" x 4" / 20 x 10 cm)

Cream Layer

¾ cup / 180 ml plus 3 tablespoons milk (whole or 2%)

1½ envelopes Knox gelatin

¾ cup / 180 ml Godiva white chocolate liqueur

Orange Layer

½ cup / 120 ml orange soda

2 tablespoons frozen orange juice concentrate (pulp-free)

1½ envelopes Knox gelatin

1 cup / 240 ml orange-flavored vodka

1 tablespoon Cointreau

O ur take on ice-cream-inspired cocktails such as the Oran-gesicle, the Dreamsicle jelly shot will take you straight back to the days of push pops. Prepare with the Checkerboard technique as shown (see Techniques section for details), or as a simple layered shot as described below.

CREAM LAYER Pour the milk into a medium saucepan and sprinkle with the gelatin. Allow the gelatin to soak for a minute or two. Heat over very low heat, stirring constantly, until gelatin is dissolved, about 5 minutes. Remove from the heat and stir in the liqueur. Pour mixture into loaf pan and refrigerate until set, about an hour. Prepare Orange Layer.

ORANGE LAYER Combine the orange soda and orange juice concentrate in a medium saucepan and sprinkle with the gelatin. Allow the gelatin to soak for a minute or two. Heat over low heat until gelatin is dissolved, stirring constantly, about 5 minutes. Remove from the heat and stir in the vodka and Cointreau. Allow mixture to cool slightly.

Ladle cooled orange mixture carefully over the set Cream Layer. Return pan to refrigerator and chill until fully set, several hours or overnight.

To serve, slice into desired shapes. Makes 18 to 24 jelly shots.

Flirtini

Difficulty: Advanced

Recommended Pan: Hemisphere molds, 9" × 9" / 23 × 23 cm square, or 9" / 23 cm round

Pineapple Layer

1⅓ cups / 315 ml pineapple juice (strained to remove solids)

2 envelopes Knox gelatin

⅔ cup / 165 ml citrus-flavored vodka

Prosecco Layer

1½ cups / 360 ml Prosecco, Champagne, or other white sparkling wine

½ cup / 120 ml water

2 tablespoons granulated sugar

2 envelopes Knox gelatin

24 to 30 maraschino cherries and edible gold leaf for garnish, if desired

The girliest of girlie drinks steps right up into jelly shot form with a maraschino cherry and edible gold leaf garnish. Drama aside, Flirtini jelly shot may also be prepared as a simple layered shot with equally delectable results.

PINEAPPLE LAYER Pour the pineapple juice into a medium saucepan and sprinkle with the gelatin. Allow the gelatin to soak for a minute or two. Heat over low heat, stirring constantly, until gelatin is fully dissolved, about 5 minutes. Remove from the heat and add the vodka, stirring well to blend. Pour mixture into hemisphere molds or pan and refrigerate until set, 1 to 2 hours. Prepare Prosecco Layer.

PROSECCO LAYER Combine the Prosecco, water, and sugar in a medium saucepan and sprinkle with the gelatin. Allow the gelatin to soak for a minute or two. Heat over very low heat, stirring constantly, until gelatin is dissolved, about 5 minutes. (Take care to heat over very low heat to avoid overheating the alcohol.) Mixture will initially be foamy, but the foam will diminish. Strain to remove any gelatin solids.

If maraschino garnish is desired, slice the bottom off each cherry. This provides the cherries with a flat surface to rest on, which will help them stay vertical instead of toppling over. If setting the jelly shots in a pan, pour the Prosecco mixture over the set pineapple layer, and add the cherries at desired intervals. If setting in a mold, place a maraschino cherry in each mold cavity. Carefully return pan/mold to refrigerator and chill until fully set, several hours or overnight.

To serve, cut into desired shapes or unmold shots. Garnish each jelly shot with edible gold leaf flakes, if desired. Makes 24 to 30 jelly shots.

French 75

Difficulty: Intermediate
Recommended Pan: 1–pound loaf pan (approximately 8" x 4" / 20 x 10 cm)

⅔ cup / 165 ml Lemon Syrup (see recipe on page 197)

⅔ cup / 165 ml Champagne, Prosecco, or other white sparkling wine

2 envelopes Knox gelatin

⅔ cup / 165 ml cognac

Lemon zest for garnish, if desired

The cocktail inspiration for the French 75 jelly shot is known to pack a bang. It is, after all, named for a French World War I Howitzer artillery piece! There is some discussion in bartending circles over whether the correct base liquor is gin or cognac—we prefer the cognac version.

COMBINE THE LEMON syrup and Champagne in a medium saucepan and sprinkle with the gelatin. Allow the gelatin to soak for a minute or two. Heat over very low heat, stirring constantly, until gelatin is fully dissolved, about 5 minutes. (Take care to use very low heat to avoid overheating the alcohol.) Remove from heat, and stir in the cognac. Pour the mixture into loaf pan and chill until fully set, several hours or overnight.

To serve, cut into desired shapes. Garnish with lemon zest, if desired. Makes 18 to 24 jelly shots.

Fuzzy Navel

Difficulty: Intermediate
Recommended Pan: 9" × 9" / 23 × 23 cm
square or 9" / 23 cm round

Peach Layer

¾ cup / 180 ml peach juice or peach
nectar (strained to remove solids)
1 envelope Knox gelatin
¼ cup / 60 ml peach schnapps

Orange Layer

1⅓ cups / 315 ml orange juice
(strained to remove solids)
2 envelopes Knox gelatin
⅔ cup / 165 ml peach schnapps

While we love the subtle variation between the peach and the orange layers, this recipe can be prepared combined, rather than layered. Just mix together all the juices, sprinkle with the gelatin, and heat as directed, adding the liquor at the end.

PEACH LAYER Pour the peach juice into a small saucepan and sprinkle with the gelatin. Allow the gelatin to soak for a minute or two. Heat on low, stirring constantly, until the gelatin is fully dissolved, about 5 minutes. Remove from the heat and add the schnapps, stirring well to blend. Pour the mixture into pan and refrigerate until fully set, at least one hour. Prepare Orange Layer.

ORANGE LAYER Pour the orange juice into a medium saucepan and sprinkle with the gelatin. Allow the gelatin to soak for a minute or so. Heat on low, stirring constantly, until gelatin is fully dissolved, about 5 minutes. Remove from the heat and add the schnapps, stirring well to blend. Allow mixture to cool slightly. Pour orange mixture over the set Peach Layer. Return to the refrigerator and chill until fully set, several hours or overnight.

To serve, cut into desired shapes with knife or cookie cutter (as shown). Makes 24 to 30 jelly shots.

Gimlet

Difficulty: Intermediate
Recommended Pan: 1–pound loaf pan
(approximately 8" x 4" / 20 x 10 cm)

⅔ cup / 165 ml Lime Syrup
   (see recipe on page 197), or
   Rose's lime juice
⅔ cup / 165 ml water
2 envelopes Knox gelatin
⅔ cup / 165 ml gin
Lime zest for garnish, if desired

The gimlet—such a hotbed of controversy! Even the appropriate garnish is contested within the Test Kitchen. Hazelnut or lime wedge? (A hazelnut being the appropriate garnish in the upper Midwestern U.S. . . .) To further fuel the debate, über-traditionalist gimlet drinkers would characterize our version as a Gin Rickey, due to our preference for fresh lime syrup over Rose's. All we can say is, garnish and lime your Gimlet jelly shot as you see fit. To prepare as shown, use the Cloudy Day technique (see Techniques section for details).

COMBINE THE LIME syrup and water in a medium saucepan and sprinkle with the gelatin. Allow the gelatin to soak for a minute or two. Heat over very low heat, stirring constantly, until gelatin is fully dissolved, about 5 minutes. Remove from heat and stir in the gin. Pour the mixture into loaf pan and refrigerate until fully set, several hours or overnight.

To serve, slice into desired shapes. Garnish with lime zest, if desired. Makes 24 to 36 small jelly shots.

Gin & Juice

Difficulty: Easy
Recommended Pan: 1–pound loaf pan
(approximately 8" x 4" / 20 x 10 cm)

1⅓ cups / 315 ml grapefruit juice
(strained to remove solids)

⅔ cup / 165 ml orange juice
(strained to remove solids)

2 tablespoons Simple Syrup
(see page 198 for recipe) or agave
nectar, plus additional, if desired

2½ envelopes Knox gelatin

⅔ cup / 165 ml gin

Simple and fabulously fresh-tasting. We discovered while formulating this recipe that grapefruit juice can become a bit intense when gelantinized. So we tempered the grapefruit with a little orange juice—just enough to dial down the pucker factor a bit, but not enough to taste the orange. For a Greyhound, substitute vodka for the gin (note that a little extra sweetener may be needed).

COMBINE BOTH JUICES and simple syrup in a medium saucepan and sprinkle with the gelatin. Allow the gelatin to soak for a minute or two. Heat over low heat, stirring constantly, until gelatin is dissolved, about 5 minutes. Remove from the heat and add the gin, stirring well to blend. Taste and add more sweetener, if desired. Pour mixture into loaf pan and refrigerate until fully set, several hours or overnight.

To serve, cut into desired shapes. Makes 18 to 24 jelly shots.

Gin & Tonic

Difficulty: Easy
Recommended Pan: 1–pound loaf pan
(approximately 8" x 4" / 20 x 10 cm)

1⅓ cups / 315 ml tonic water

1 tablespoon freshly squeezed lime
juice, or Rose's lime juice, to taste

1 to 2 tablespoons Simple Syrup
(see recipe on page 198) or
agave nectar

2 envelopes Knox gelatin

⅔ cup / 165 ml gin

Small lime wedges for garnish

We love a gin and tonic. It is truly the perfect mid-after-noon-watch-the-sailboats-drift-by drink—even if you have to make up the sailboat part and just watch the world drift by. Gin & Tonic jelly shot inspires the same ardor, with its delicate texture and tonic-y goodness. Serve each jelly shot with a tiny lime wedge, to squeeze over the top, for extra authenticity.

COMBINE THE TONIC, lime juice, and simple syrup in a small saucepan and sprinkle with the gelatin. Allow the gelatin to soak for a minute or two. Heat over low heat, stirring constantly, until gelatin is dissolved, about 5 minutes. (Mixture will be very foamy, but this will diminish.) Remove from the heat and stir in the gin. If necessary, strain to remove any gelatin solids.

Pour mixture into loaf pan and refrigerate until fully set, several hours or overnight.

To serve, cut into desired shapes. Garnish each jelly shot with a lime wedge to squeeze over the shot. Makes 18 to 24 jelly shots.

Grasshopper

Difficulty: Easy

Recommended Pan: 9" × 9" / 23 × 23 cm square or 9" / 23 cm round

1 cup / 240 ml milk (whole or 2%)

3 envelopes Knox gelatin

1 cup / 240 ml Godiva white chocolate liqueur

1 cup / 240 ml vanilla-flavored vodka

3 to 4 tablespoons crème de menthe liqueur (to taste)

White chocolate shavings for garnish, if needed

Mild and minty, the Grasshopper jelly shot is ideal to serve at an afternoon wedding reception or tea with the Queen. In our gelatin interpretation of the classic dessert cocktail, we substitute white chocolate liqueur for white crème de cacao. Why? Because it's yummy.

POUR THE MILK into a medium saucepan and sprinkle with the gelatin. Allow the gelatin to soak for a minute or two. Heat over low heat until gelatin is dissolved, stirring constantly, about 5 minutes. (Mixture will be quite thick initially.) Remove from the heat and stir in the white chocolate liqueur, and then the vodka, stirring well to blend. Add the crème de menthe. Strain mixture through a fine sieve to remove any gelatin solids. Pour into pan and refrigerate until fully set, several hours or overnight.

To serve, cut into desired shapes with a knife or cookie cutter (as shown, cut with a fluted, round cookie cutter, then cut in half). Garnish with white chocolate shavings, if desired. Makes 24 to 30 jelly shots.

Hurricane

Difficulty: Easy
Recommended Pan: 9" × 9" / 23 × 23 cm
square, or 9" / 23 cm round

½ cup / 120 ml passion fruit nectar

½ cup / 120 ml freshly squeezed
  orange juice (strained to
  remove solids)

⅓ cup / 75 ml freshly squeezed lime
  juice (strained to remove solids)

½ cup / 120 ml grenadine

2½ envelopes Knox gelatin

½ cup / 120 ml white rum

½ cup / 120 ml dark rum

Orange segments for garnish,
  if desired

Whip up your own Mardi Gras celebration with a platter of Hurricane jelly shots (Mardi Gras beads optional).

COMBINE THE PASSION fruit nectar, orange juice, lime juice, and grenadine in a medium saucepan and sprinkle with the gelatin. Allow the gelatin to soak for a minute or two. Heat over low heat, stirring constantly, until gelatin is fully dissolved, about 5 minutes. Remove from the heat and stir in both rums. Pour mixture into pan and refrigerate until fully set, several hours or overnight.

To serve, cut into desired shapes. Garnish with orange segments, if desired. Makes 24 to 30 jelly shots.

Jack Rose

Difficulty: Intermediate
Recommended Pan: 1–pound loaf pan
(approximately 8" x 4" / 20 x 10 cm)

¾ cup / 180 ml Lemon Syrup
  (see recipe on page 197)
2 envelopes Knox gelatin
¼ cup / 60 ml pomegranate juice
1 cup / 240 ml applejack brandy
Orange zest for garnish, if desired

This jelly shot's sweet-tart kick is bolstered by a shot of applejack brandy. One of the true, but relatively unknown, classic cocktails, the Jack Rose makes an appearance in Ernest Hemingway's novel *The Sun Also Rises*. Lady Brett Ashley would certainly approve!

POUR THE LEMON syrup into a medium saucepan and sprinkle with the gelatin. Allow gelatin to soak for a few minutes. Heat over very low heat until gelatin is dissolved, stirring constantly, about 5 minutes. Remove from the heat and add the pomegranate juice and then the applejack, stirring well to blend. Pour into loaf pan and refrigerate until fully set, several hours or overnight.

To serve, cut into desired shapes. Garnish with orange zest, if desired. Makes 18 to 24 jelly shots.

Kamikaze

Difficulty: Intermediate
Recommended Pan: 1–pound loaf pan
(approximately 8" x 4" / 20 x 10 cm)
or molds

¼ cup / 60 ml Lime Syrup
  (see recipe on page 197) or
  Rose's lime juice
½ cup / 120 ml water
2 envelopes Knox gelatin
1 cup / 240 ml vodka
¼ cup / 60 ml Cointreau
1 teaspoon Simple Syrup
  (see recipe on page 198) or
  agave nectar, if desired

Ah, memories. Say "Kamikaze" and our thoughts immediately gravitate to the Black Watch in Los Gatos, California, where bartenders have been shaking their legendary and highly potent "kamis" for decades. Black Watch Kamikazes are served in a pint glass, with a strainer and shot glasses on the side, to a throng of enthusiastic imbibers typically piled in four-deep at the bar. The Kamikaze jelly shot, served cut or molded, is just as consumable as the liquid version was back in the day.

COMBINE THE LIME syrup and water in a small saucepan and sprinkle with gelatin. Allow the gelatin to soak for a minute or two. Heat over low heat, stirring constantly, until gelatin is dissolved, about 5 minutes. (Mixture will initially be very thick.) Remove from the heat and stir in the vodka and Cointreau. Taste and add the simple syrup or agave nectar, if desired. Pour mixture into loaf pan or molds and refrigerate until fully set, several hours or overnight.

To serve, cut into desired shapes or unmold shots. Makes 18 to 24 jelly shots.

Variation: Raspberry Kamikaze

Add 3 to 4 tablespoons of raspberry schnapps when stirring in the vodka and Cointreau.

Key Lime Martini

Difficulty: Intermediate

Recommended Pan: 1–pound loaf pan (approximately 8" × 4" / 20 × 10 cm)

⅔ cup / 165 ml Key Lime Syrup (see recipe on page 197) or Rose's lime juice

¼ cup / 60 ml pineapple juice, strained to remove solids

2 envelopes Knox gelatin

⅔ cup / 165 ml vanilla-flavored vodka

⅔ cup / 165 ml Malibu coconut rum

Key lime slices or zest for garnish, if desired

The Key Lime Martini jelly shot is just as refreshing, if not quite as sweet as its pie-inspired cousin (Key Lime Pie Martini). If key limes for the Key Lime Syrup (see Syrup Recipes section) are not available, regular lime syrup or Rose's lime juice will do the trick.

COMBINE THE KEY lime syrup and pineapple juice in a medium saucepan and sprinkle with the gelatin. Allow the gelatin to soak for a minute or two. Heat over very low heat until gelatin is dissolved, stirring constantly, about 5 minutes. Remove from the heat and stir in the vodka and rum. Pour into loaf pan and refrigerate until fully set, several hours or overnight.

To serve, cut into desired shapes and garnish with lime slices or zest, if desired. Makes 18 to 24 jelly shots.

Key Lime Pie Martini

Difficulty: Intermediate

Recommended Pan: 1–pound loaf pan (approximately 8" x 4" / 20 x 10 cm)

1 cup / 240 ml Key Lime Syrup (see recipe on page 197) or Rose's lime juice

2 tablespoons Simple Syrup (see recipe on page 198)

¼ cup / 60 ml pineapple juice, strained to remove solids

3 envelopes Knox gelatin

¼ cup / 60 ml heavy cream

1 cup / 240 ml vanilla-flavored vodka

1 cup / 240 ml Malibu coconut rum

½ cup graham cracker crumbs

We like to use a standard loaf pan for this shot, cut the jelly shots into ¾- to 1-inch-square (or 2 to 2.5 cm) pieces, and plate each shot on one of its long sides. This results in a rectangular shot with a very dramatic "cream" layer on one end. The graham cracker crumb garnish enhances the pie-like experience. Dip the bottom side of the shot into the crumbs immediately before serving, or plate with a small dish of crumbs for dipping.

COMBINE THE KEY lime syrup, simple syrup and pineapple juice in a medium saucepan and sprinkle with the gelatin. Allow the gelatin to soak for a minute or two. Stir in the cream. (The cream may separate from the mixture; just keep stirring and it will eventually incorporate.) Heat over very low heat, stirring constantly, until gelatin is dissolved, about 5 minutes. Remove from the heat and stir in the vodka and rum. Pour into loaf pan and refrigerate until fully set, several hours or overnight.

As the gelatin mixture cools, the cream will rise to the top and form a separate layer, giving the completed jelly shot a very pie-like appearance.

To serve, cut into desired shapes. Immediately before serving, dip one end of each jelly shot into graham cracker crumbs, or plate the shots with a small dish of graham cracker crumbs for dipping. Makes 24 to 30 jelly shots.

Kir Royale

Difficulty: Easy

Recommended Pan: 1–pound loaf pan
(approximately 8" x 4" / 20 x 10 cm)

1½ cups / 360 ml Champagne,
   Prosecco or other white
   sparkling wine

½ cup / 120 ml water

2 tablespoons granulated sugar

2 envelopes Knox gelatin

2 tablespoons crème de cassis

Edible flowers for garnish, if desired

A lovely aperitif jelly shot, the Kir Royale is perfect on its own, or with a mixed plate of other Champagne-based jelly shots, such as Champagne Cocktail and Champagne & Liqueur. Traditionalists may garnish with lemon peel, but in this case we break with tradition and prefer an edible flower petal or nothing at all.

COMBINE THE CHAMPAGNE, water, and sugar in a medium saucepan and sprinkle with the gelatin. Allow the gelatin to soak for a minute or two. Heat over very low heat, stirring constantly, until gelatin is dissolved, about 5 minutes. (Take care to use very low heat, to avoid overheating the alcohol.) Mixture will initially be foamy, but this will diminish. Remove from the heat and strain mixture to remove any remaining gelatin solids.

Stir in the crème de cassis and pour mixture into pan. Refrigerate until fully set, several hours or overnight.

To serve, cut into desired shapes and garnish with edible flowers, if desired. Makes 18 to 24 jelly shots.

Lemon Drop

Difficulty: Intermediate
Recommended Pan: 1–pound loaf pan
(approximately 8" x 4" / 20 x 10 cm)

1 cup / 240 ml Lemon Syrup
 (see recipe on page 197)
¼ cup / 60 ml water
2 envelopes Knox gelatin
¼ cup / 60 ml Cointreau
½ cup / 120 ml vodka
Large-crystal sugar for garnish,
 if desired

P otent and as tart and lemony as their candy and cocktail inspirations, Lemon Drop jelly shots are always a sure hit. For a slightly milder—but equally potent—lemony shot, try the Lemon Meringue jelly shot.

POUR THE LEMON syrup and water into a medium saucepan and sprinkle with the gelatin. Allow the gelatin to soak for a minute or two. Heat over very low heat, stirring constantly, until gelatin is fully dissolved, about 5 minutes. Remove from the heat and add the Cointreau and vodka, stirring well to blend. Pour the mixture into loaf pan and refrigerate until fully set, several hours or overnight.

To serve, cut into desired shapes. Immediately before serving, dip one side of each jelly shot into sugar for garnish, if desired. Makes 18 to 24 jelly shots.

Lemon Meringue

Difficulty: Easy
Recommended Pan: 1–pound loaf pan
(approximately 8" x 4" / 20 x 10 cm)

1 cup / 240 ml limoncello liqueur

2 envelopes Knox gelatin

½ cup / 120 ml citrus-flavored vodka

½ cup / 120 ml white crème de
   cacao liqueur

Lemon zest for garnish, if desired

Much like its pastry inspiration, Lemon Meringue jelly shot provides a subtle lemon flavor and sweet meringue-like taste, courtesy of the white crème de cacao.

POUR THE LIMONCELLO into a medium saucepan and sprinkle with the gelatin. Allow the gelatin to soak for a minute or two. Heat over low heat until gelatin is dissolved, stirring constantly, about 5 minutes. (Take care to use very low heat to avoid overheating the alcohol.) Remove from the heat and add the vodka and crème de cacao, stirring well to blend. Pour the mixture into loaf pan and refrigerate until fully set, several hours or overnight.

To serve, cut into desired shapes. Garnish with lemon zest, if desired. Makes 18 to 32 jelly shots.

Long Island Iced Tea

Difficulty: Intermediate
Recommended Pan: 9" × 9"/23 × 23 cm
square, or 9"/23 cm round

1½ cups / 360 ml Diet Coke

¼ cup / 60 ml Lemon Syrup
(see recipe on page 197)

3 envelopes Knox gelatin

¼ cup / 60 ml vodka

¼ cup / 60 ml gin

¼ cup / 60 ml rum

¼ cup / 60 ml tequila

¼ cup / 60 ml Triple Sec

25 bamboo skewers and small lemon
wedges for serving, if desired

This kitchen-sink cocktail goes down just as smoothly in gelatin form, and sets the perfect tone for a barbecue or other warm-weather gathering. Try serving the jelly shots threaded onto bamboo cocktail skewers with a small lemon wedge.

COMBINE THE DIET Coke and lemon syrup in a medium saucepan and sprinkle with the gelatin. Allow the gelatin to soak for a minute or two. Heat over very low heat until the gelatin is dissolved, stirring constantly, about 5 minutes. Remove from the heat and add the liquors, stirring well to blend. Pour into pan and refrigerate until fully set, several hours or overnight.

To serve, cut into small circles or squares. Thread a small lemon wedge onto each bamboo skewer, followed by two small jelly shots. Refrigerate until ready to serve. Makes 25 skewers, or approximately 50 small (½-inch / 12 mm) jelly shots.

Lynchburg Lemonade

Difficulty: Intermediate

Recommended Pan: 1–pound loaf pan
(approximately 8" x 4" / 20 x 10 cm)

½ cup / 120 ml lemon-lime soda
½ cup / 120 ml Lemon Syrup
  (see recipe on page 197)
2 envelopes Knox gelatin
½ cup / 120 ml Jack Daniel's whiskey
½ cup / 120 ml Cointreau

Named for the Tennessee town that is home to the Jack Daniel's whiskey distillery, Lynchburg Lemonade is a powerful but amazingly palatable concoction of lemon and whiskey. Similar in taste to its sibling, the whiskey sour, it has a sophisticated, subtle orange hint courtesy of the Cointreau.

COMBINE THE SODA and lemon syrup in a medium saucepan and sprinkle with the gelatin. Allow the gelatin to soak for a minute or two. Heat over very low heat until gelatin is dissolved, stirring constantly, about 5 minutes. Remove from the heat and stir in the whiskey and Cointreau, stirring well to blend. Pour mixture into loaf pan and refrigerate until fully set, several hours or overnight.

To serve, cut into desired shapes. Makes 18 to 24 jelly shots.

Madras

Difficulty: Intermediate
Recommended Pan: 1–pound loaf pan
(approximately 8" x 4" / 20 x 10 cm)

Cranberry Layer

¾ cup / 180 ml cranberry juice
 cocktail

2 tablespoons cranberry juice
 concentrate

2 envelopes Knox gelatin

¾ cup / 180 ml vodka

Orange Layer

½ cup / 120 ml orange juice
 (strained to remove solids)

½ envelope Knox gelatin

Pop your collar for this perfect jelly shot accompaniment to plaid shorts and Lily Pulitzer sundresses. Serve the refreshing Madras jelly shots solo, or with their kissing cousins, the Sea Breeze jelly shots (made with grapefruit juice instead of orange juice). We prepared the cranberry layer using the Bubble technique (see Techniques section for details).

CRANBERRY LAYER Combine the cranberry juice cocktail and concentrate in a small saucepan and sprinkle with the gelatin. Allow the gelatin to soak for a minute or two. Heat over low heat, stirring constantly, until gelatin is fully dissolved, about 5 minutes. Remove from the heat and stir in the vodka. Pour into loaf pan and chill until fully set, several hours. Prepare Orange Layer.

ORANGE LAYER Pour the orange juice into a small saucepan and sprinkle with the gelatin. Allow the gelatin to soak for a minute or two. Heat over low heat, stirring constantly, until gelatin is fully dissolved, about 5 minutes. Remove from the heat and allow to cool slightly. Pour slightly cooled orange mixture over the set Cranberry Layer in loaf pan. Return pan to refrigerator and chill until fully set, several hours or overnight.

To serve, cut into desired shapes. Makes 18 to 24 jelly shots.

Mai Tai

Difficulty: Intermediate

Recommended Pan: 1–pound loaf pan (approximately 8" x 4" / 20 x 10 cm)

1 cup / 240 ml orange juice (strained to remove solids)

2 tablespoons Lime Syrup (see recipe on page 197)

2 envelopes Knox gelatin

¼ cup / 60 ml dark rum

¼ cup / 60 ml white rum

¼ cup / 60 ml Cointreau

1 tablespoon crème de almond liqueur

Dash Simple Syrup (see recipe on page 198) or agave nectar, if desired

Lime zest or small segments of pineapple, orange, and maraschino cherry for garnish, if desired

A tropical delight, the Mai Tai cocktail never fails to please. Mai Tai jelly shot follows in the footsteps of its classic cocktail inspiration. The Mai Tai is traditionally made with orgeat, a syrup made from almonds, sugar, and rose water or orange-flower water. We substituted a little crème de almond liqueur for the orgeat in this recipe.

COMBINE THE ORANGE juice and lime syrup in a small saucepan and sprinkle with the gelatin. Allow the gelatin to soak for a minute or two. Heat over very low heat until gelatin has fully dissolved, about 5 minutes. Remove from the heat and stir in both rums, Cointreau, and crème de almond. Taste and add sweetener, if desired. Pour mixture into loaf pan and refrigerate until fully set, several hours or overnight.

To serve, cut into desired shapes. Garnish with lime zest or small segments of pineapple, orange, and maraschino cherry for garnish, if desired. Makes 18 to 24 jelly shots.

Manhattan

Difficulty: Intermediate
Recommended Pan: 1–pound loaf pan
(approximately 8" x 4" / 20 x 10 cm)

⅔ cup / 165 ml Bitters Syrup
  (see page 196 for recipe)
2 envelopes Knox gelatin
⅔ cup / 165 ml bourbon
⅔ cup Italian sweet vermouth
Maraschino cherries, diced small
  for garnish, if desired

O ur interpretation of the Manhattan has a southern accent, in that it uses bourbon instead of rye whiskey (New York has always been a rye town). Does that mean our Manhattan is more like a Knoxville? Certainly not. The subtle smoke pattern in the finished jelly shots is a result of the interaction of the gelatin, water, and bourbon in the cooking process.

POUR THE BITTERS syrup into a medium saucepan and sprinkle with the gelatin. Allow the gelatin to soak for a minute or two. Heat over very low heat until gelatin is dissolved, stirring constantly, about 5 minutes. Remove from the heat and stir in the bourbon and the sweet vermouth. Pour into loaf pan and refrigerate until fully set, several hours or overnight.

To serve, cut into desired shapes and garnish with the diced maraschino, if desired. Makes 18 to 24 jelly shots.

Margarita

Difficulty: Intermediate
Recommended Pan: 1–pound loaf pan
(approximately 8" x 4" / 20 x 10 cm)

1 cup / 240 ml Lime Syrup
  (see recipe on page 197) or
  Rose's lime juice

2 envelopes Knox gelatin

¾ cup / 180 ml 100% agave tequila

½ cup / 120 ml Cointreau

1 tablespoon Simple Syrup
  (see recipe on page 198) or
  agave nectar, if desired

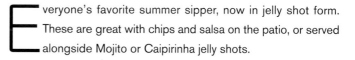

Everyone's favorite summer sipper, now in jelly shot form. These are great with chips and salsa on the patio, or served alongside Mojito or Caipirinha jelly shots.

POUR THE LIME syrup into a medium saucepan and sprinkle with the gelatin. Allow the gelatin to soak for a minute or two. Heat over very low heat until gelatin is dissolved, stirring constantly, about 5 minutes. Remove from the heat and stir in the tequila and Cointreau. Taste mixture and add sweetener if desired. Pour mixture into loaf pan and refrigerate until fully set, several hours or overnight.

To serve, cut into desired shapes. Makes 18 to 24 jelly shots.

Variation: Strawberry Margarita

Swap out ½ cup / 120 ml of lime syrup for the same measure of Strawberry Syrup (see recipe on page 198). A good quality purchased strawberry syrup, such as Monin brand, will also do the trick. Feeling frisky? Experiment with other fruit flavored syrups, such as blackberry or mango.

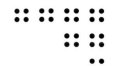

Melon Ball

Difficulty: Easy
Recommended Pan: 1–pound loaf pan
(approximately 8" x 4" / 20 x 10 cm)

1 cup / 240 ml pineapple juice
  (strained to remove solids)
2 envelopes Knox gelatin
⅔ cup / 105 ml Midori
⅓ cup / 75 ml vodka

This mild, patio-friendly recipe gets its bright melon taste and verdant tint from Midori liqueur. Try skewering with melon rounds and other fruit for an alternative to a brunch aperitif.

POUR THE PINEAPPLE juice into a medium saucepan and sprinkle with the gelatin. Allow the gelatin to soak for a minute or two. Heat over very low heat until gelatin is dissolved, stirring constantly, about 5 minutes. Remove from the heat and add the Midori and vodka, stirring well to blend. Pour the mixture into loaf pan and refrigerate until fully set, several hours or overnight.

To serve, cut into desired shapes. Makes 18 to 24 jelly shots.

Mojito

Difficulty: Intermediate
Recommended Pan: 1–pound loaf pan
(approximately 8" x 4" / 20 x 10 cm)

1¼ cups / 300 ml Mojito Syrup
  (see recipe on page 197)

2 envelopes Knox gelatin

1 cup / 240 ml white rum

2 teaspoons finely chopped fresh
  mint leaves, plus additional for
  garnish, if desired

Everyone's favorite Cuban highball interpreted in jelly shot form. As minty and refreshing as the cocktail original, these are perfect served solo or grouped with other rum-based treats.

POUR THE MOJITO syrup into a medium saucepan and sprinkle with the gelatin. Allow the gelatin to soak for a minute or two. Heat over low heat, stirring constantly, until gelatin is fully dissolved, about 5 minutes. Remove from the heat and stir in the rum and chopped mint. Pour the mixture into loaf pan and refrigerate until fully set, several hours or overnight.

To serve, cut into desired shapes. Garnish with chopped fresh mint, if desired. Makes 18 to 24 jelly shots.

Mint Julep

Difficulty: Easy
Recommended Pan: 1–pound loaf pan (approximately 8" × 4" / 20 × 10 cm)
Implements: Cocktail shaker and cocktail muddler

½ cup / 10 g fresh mint leaves

1 cup / 240 ml water

Ice cubes

½ cup / 120 ml Simple Syrup
  (see recipe on page 198)

2 envelopes Knox gelatin

½ cup / 120 ml bourbon

Mint leaves for garnish, if desired

A harbinger of spring, the mint julep is the traditional beverage for Kentucky Derby, which is run the first weekend in May each year. For best results, wear a big, beribboned hat while preparing and consuming this jelly shot. It also doesn't hurt to use your finest bourbon. You can garnish these simply with slivers of fresh mint, or thread each jelly shot on a silver skewer with a small mint leaf.

MUDDLE THE MINT leaves in the cocktail shaker (reserving 12 small leaves for garnish). Add the water, fill shaker with ice cubes, and shake vigorously. Strain liquid through a fine mesh strainer and set aside.

Pour the simple syrup into a small saucepan and sprinkle with the gelatin. Allow the gelatin to soak for a minute or two. Heat over low heat, stirring constantly, until the gelatin has dissolved, about 5 minutes. Remove from heat and stir in the bourbon. Gradually add the reserved mint water to the gelatin mixture, stirring well to blend. Pour into loaf pan and chill until fully set, several hours or overnight.

To serve, cut into desired shapes. Cut the mint leaves into slivers, and garnish the jelly shots, if desired. Makes 18 to 24 jelly shots.

Mudslide

Difficulty: Easy
Recommended Pan: 1–pound loaf pan
(approximately 8" x 4" / 20 x 10 cm)

½ cup / 120 ml milk (whole or 2%)

2 envelopes Knox gelatin

½ cup / 120 ml Kahlúa coffee liqueur

½ cup / 120 ml Baileys Irish
   cream liqueur

½ cup / 120 ml vodka

Many variations exist for the frozen Mudslide cocktail, and the Mudslide jelly shot is just as versatile. Mix it up by replacing half of the Kahlúa called for in the recipe below with the liqueur of your choice, such as butterscotch schnapps or crème de menthe.

POUR THE MILK into a small saucepan and sprinkle with the gelatin. Allow the gelatin to soak for a minute or two. Heat over low heat, stirring constantly, until gelatin is fully dissolved, about 5 minutes. (Mixture will be quite thick initially.) Remove from the heat and add the Kahlúa and Baileys, and then the vodka, stirring well to blend. Pour mixture into loaf pan and chill until fully set, several hours or overnight.

To serve, cut into desired shapes. Makes 18 to 24 jelly shots.

Negroni

Difficulty: Easy
Recommended Pan: 1–pound loaf pan
(approximately 8" x 4" / 20 × 10 cm)

1 cup / 240 ml water

1 (1 x 2-inch / 2.5 x 5 cm) strip of
   orange zest

2 envelopes Knox gelatin

⅓ cup / 75 ml Campari

⅓ cup / 75 ml sweet Italian red
   vermouth

⅓ cup / 75 ml Hendrick's gin

Edible gold leaf flakes and additional
   orange zest for garnish, if desired

Pleasantly bitter, ruby red, and braced with gin, the Negroni cocktail is no shrinking wallflower. Although the cocktail was purportedly invented in Florence, Italy, we enjoyed our first Negroni on a trip to Venice, and find the cocktail is everything a trip to Venice ought to be: surprising at first sip and comfortably familiar by the end. Garnish the Negroni jelly shot in the opulent fashion of the Doge's Palace, topped with edible gold leaf and a healthy dose of orange zest.

COMBINE THE WATER and orange zest in a medium saucepan and sprinkle with the gelatin. Allow the gelatin to soak for a minute or two. Heat over low heat, stirring constantly, until gelatin has dissolved, about 5 minutes. Remove from the heat and discard orange zest. Stir in the Campari, vermouth, and gin. Pour mixture into loaf pan and chill until fully set, several hours or overnight.

To serve, cut into desired shapes. Garnish with orange zest and edible gold leaf flakes, if desired. Makes 18 to 24 jelly shots.

Oasis Breeze

Difficulty: Easy
Recommended Pan: 9" × 9" / 23 × 23 cm square or 9" / 23 cm round

1 cup / 240 ml pineapple juice (strained to remove solids)

¼ cup / 60 ml cranberry juice cocktail

2½ envelopes Knox gelatin

1 cup / 240 ml Malibu coconut rum

¼ cup / 60 ml dark rum

1 teaspoon grenadine

Sliced pineapple and shredded coconut for garnish, if desired

The cocktail inspiration for this light, fresh, and amazingly delicious jelly shot is a riff on the Malibu Bay Breeze, which was concocted by our favorite bar captain, Meera of Royal Caribbean cruise lines, in the spring of 2010. Meera is currently serving on the Oasis of the Seas, hence the name of this jelly shot.

COMBINE THE PINEAPPLE and cranberry juices in a medium saucepan and sprinkle with the gelatin. Allow the gelatin to soak for a minute or two. Heat over low heat, stirring constantly, until gelatin is fully dissolved, about 5 minutes. Add both rums and the grenadine, stirring well to blend. Pour into pan and refrigerate until fully set, several hours or overnight.

To serve, cut into desired shapes and garnish with pineapple and coconut, if desired. Makes 18 to 24 jelly shots.

Old Fashioned

Recommended Pan: 1–pound loaf pan
(approximately 8" x 4" / 20 x 10 cm)

⅔ cup / 165 ml soda water

⅔ cup / 165 ml Bitters Syrup
(see recipe on page 196)

2 tablespoons maraschino
cherry juice

2 envelopes Knox gelatin

⅔ cup / 165 ml bourbon or
scotch whiskey

Orange slices and maraschino
cherries for garnish, if desired

Another classic cocktail surrounded by controversy—to muddle, or not to muddle? The fruit, that is. We are big muddlers, and as such have included maraschino cherry juice in our jelly shot interpretation. If you are an anti-muddling Old Fashioned aficionado, feel free to leave it out.

COMBINE THE SODA water, bitters syrup, and cherry juice in a small saucepan and sprinkle with the gelatin. Allow the gelatin to soak for a minute or two. Heat over very low heat until gelatin is dissolved, stirring constantly, about 5 minutes. Remove from the heat and add the whisky, stirring well to blend. Pour into pan and refrigerate until fully set, several hours or overnight.

Cut the orange and cherries into small slivers for garnish. To serve, cut the set gelatin into desired shapes and garnish as desired. Makes 18 to 24 jelly shots.

143
TEST
Jelly Shot KITCHEN

Peanut Butter & Jelly Martini

Difficulty: Intermediate

Recommended Pan: 1–pound loaf pan (approximately 8" × 4" / 20 × 10 cm)

¼ cup / 60 ml Strawberry Syrup (see recipe on page 198) or purchased strawberry syrup, such as Monin brand

½ cup / 120 ml water

2½ envelopes Knox gelatin

¾ cup / 180 ml vodka

½ cup / 120 ml Frangelico hazelnut liqueur

½ cup / 120 ml crème de cassis (black currant liqueur)

Not just a lunchbox staple, this PB&J is strictly for the big boys. The jelly shot, like its cocktail inspiration, gets its nutty taste from Frangelico liqueur. Prefer your PB&Js chunky-style? Garnish with chopped peanuts.

COMBINE THE STRAWBERRY syrup and water in a medium saucepan and sprinkle with the gelatin. Allow the gelatin to soak for a minute or two. Heat over low heat, stirring constantly, until gelatin is dissolved, about 5 minutes. Remove from the heat and add the vodka and both liqueurs, stirring well to blend. Pour mixture into loaf pan and refrigerate until fully set, several hours or overnight.

To serve, cut into desired shapes. Makes 18 to 24 jelly shots.

Pimm's Cup

Difficulty: Intermediate
Recommended Pan: 1–pound loaf pan (approximately 8" x 4" / 20 x 10 cm)
Implements: Large cocktail shaker and cocktail muddler

4 strawberries

1 orange slice (about 1-inch / 2.5 cm thick), coarsely chopped

2 large sprigs fresh mint

1 (1-inch / 2.5 cm) piece cucumber, coarsely chopped

¾ cup / 180 ml Pimm's No. 1 Cup

6 ice cubes

⅔ cup / 165 ml ginger ale

⅔ cup / 165 ml Lemon Syrup (see recipe on page 197)

2 envelopes Knox gelatin

Slivers of cucumber, strawberry, orange, and mint for garnish, if desired

This Wimbledon cocktail favorite is a veritable fruit salad of summertime deliciousness. Pimm's No. 1 is a gin-based aperitif flavored with citrus and spices. Several ingredients in this cocktail are hotly debated, including the appropriate soda and fruit garnish. As reflected below, we land on the side of lemon-spiked ginger ale, with strawberries, please. This recipe will work equally well with lemon-lime soda replacing the ginger ale, and your favorite fruits for muddling and garnish.

MUDDLE TOGETHER THE strawberries, orange, mint, and chopped cucumber in a large cocktail shaker. Add the Pimm's and the ice cubes and shake vigorously. Strain liquid through a fine mesh strainer and set aside. (You should have approximately ⅔ cup / 165 ml liquid.)

Combine the ginger ale and lemon syrup in a medium saucepan and sprinkle with the gelatin. Allow the gelatin to soak for a minute or two. Heat over very low heat, stirring constantly, until gelatin is fully dissolved, about 5 minutes. Remove from the heat and add the reserved Pimm's liquid, stirring well to blend. Pour into pan and chill until fully set, several hours or overnight.

To serve, cut into rectangles. To garnish, peel "ribbons" from cucumber using a vegetable peeler. The ribbons should be about 6 inches / 15 cm long for easy handling. Group the slivered fruit and mint as desired, and tie each bundle with a cucumber ribbon. Trim the ribbon ends to desired length. Place a fruit bundle on each jelly shot. Makes 12 to 18 jelly shots.

Piña Colada

Difficulty: Easy
Recommended Pan: 1–pound loaf pan
(approximately 8" x 4" / 20 x 10 cm)

1 cup / 240 ml canned pineapple
  juice (strained to remove solids)
¼ cup / 60 ml cream of coconut,
  such as Coco Lopez
2 envelopes Knox gelatin
¾ cup / 180 ml Malibu coconut rum
Shredded coconut for garnish,
  if desired

This was our very first jelly shot recipe, and it is still a favorite with our guests. Cut the jelly shots into triangles and serve on a clear plate for a "sailboat" effect.

COMBINE THE PINEAPPLE juice and cream of coconut in a medium saucepan and sprinkle with the gelatin. Allow the gelatin to soak for a minute or two. Heat over low heat, stirring constantly, until gelatin is fully dissolved, about 5 minutes. Remove from the heat and stir in the Malibu rum. Pour mixture into loaf pan and refrigerate until fully set, several hours or overnight.

To serve, cut into desired shapes. Garnish each shot with shredded coconut, if desired. Makes 18 to 24 jelly shots.

Pink Squirrel

Difficulty: Easy
Recommended Pan: 1–pound loaf pan
(approximately 8" x 4" / 20 x 10 cm)
or molds

⅔ cup / 165 ml milk (whole or 2%)

2 envelopes Knox gelatin

⅔ cup / 165 ml Godiva white
chocolate liqueur

⅔ cup / 165 ml vanilla-flavored vodka

2 to 3 tablespoons crème de almond
liqueur (to taste)

White chocolate shavings for garnish,
if desired

The Pink Squirrel cocktail is traditionally made with white crème de cacao. In this jelly shot interpretation, we substitute Godiva white chocolate liqueur, but either may be used. The crème de almond, also known as crème de noyaux, provides the distinctive pink color.

POUR THE MILK into a medium saucepan and sprinkle with the gelatin. Allow the gelatin to soak for a minute or two. Heat over low heat until gelatin is dissolved, stirring constantly, about 5 minutes. (Mixture will be quite thick to start.) Remove from the heat and stir in the white chocolate liqueur, vodka, and the crème de almond. Strain mixture to remove any gelatin solids. Pour strained mixture into loaf pan or molds and refrigerate until fully set, several hours or overnight.

To serve, cut into desired shapes or unmold shots. Garnish each shot with white chocolate shavings, if desired. Makes 18 to 24 jelly shots.

Pomegranate Martini

Difficulty: Easy
Recommended Pan: 1–pound loaf pan
(approximately 8" x 4" / 20 x 10 cm)

1 cup / 240 ml pomegranate juice

2½ envelopes Knox gelatin

1 cup / 240 ml vodka

½ cup / 120 ml Cointreau

Flavored cocktail rimming sugar or
    lime zest for garnish, if desired

Holiday pizzazz, antioxidants, AND intoxicating properties? Amazingly, the Pomegranate Martini really does have it all. Try serving on a mixed plate with Sweet and Sour Apple Martini jelly shots. Garnish as shown here, dipped in cranberry-flavored cocktail sugar, or sprinkled with lime zest.

POUR THE POMEGRANATE juice into a medium saucepan and sprinkle with the gelatin. Allow the gelatin to soak for a minute or two. Heat over low heat, stirring constantly, until gelatin is dissolved, about 5 minutes. Remove from the heat and stir in the vodka and Cointreau. Pour mixture into loaf pan or molds and chill until set, several hours or overnight.

To serve, cut into desired shapes and unmold shots. Garnish as desired. Makes 18 to 24 jelly shots.

Sambuca

Difficulty: Easy

Recommended Pan: 1–pound loaf pan (approximately 8" x 4" / 20 x 10 cm)

1 cup / 240 ml water

2 envelopes Knox gelatin

1 cup / 240 ml sambuca liqueur

We find that one is either a black licorice fan or foe, and never the twain shall meet. If you are a fan, you will love the jelly shot interpretation of the anise-flavored liqueur. Either the clear or black version (as shown here) of sambuca liqueur may be used.

POUR THE WATER into a medium saucepan and sprinkle with the gelatin. Allow the gelatin to soak for a minute or two. Heat over very low heat until gelatin is dissolved, stirring constantly, about 5 minutes. Remove from the heat and add the sambuca, stirring well to blend. Pour mixture into loaf pan and refrigerate until fully set, several hours or overnight.

To serve, cut into desired shapes. Makes approximately 18 to 24 jelly shots.

Sea Breeze

Difficulty: Intermediate

Recommended Pan: 1–pound loaf pan (approximately 8" × 4" / 20 × 10 cm)

Cranberry Layer
¾ cup / 180 ml cranberry
  juice cocktail
2 tablespoons cranberry juice
  concentrate
1½ envelopes Knox gelatin
¾ cup / 180 ml vodka

Grapefruit Layer
½ cup / 120 ml grapefruit juice
½ envelope Knox gelatin

Traditionally, the Sea Breeze cocktail is prepared with a larger quantity of grapefruit juice and just a splash of cranberry as a topper. In our cocktails and our Sea Breeze jelly shot, we prefer a cranberry-based cocktail with just a hint of citrus. Directions for a two-layered jelly shot follow—for extra oomph, prepare as a four-layer shot by dividing each gelatin mixture in half.

CRANBERRY LAYER Combine the cranberry juice cocktail and concentrate in a small saucepan and sprinkle with the gelatin. Allow the gelatin to soak for a minute or two. Heat over low heat, stirring constantly, until gelatin is fully dissolved, about 5 minutes. Remove from the heat and add the vodka, stirring well to blend. Pour mixture into loaf pan and refrigerate until fully set, one to two hours. Prepare Grapefruit Layer.

GRAPEFRUIT LAYER Pour the grapefruit juice into a small saucepan and sprinkle with the gelatin. Allow the gelatin to soak for a minute or two. Heat over low heat, stirring constantly, until gelatin is fully dissolved, about 5 minutes. Remove from the heat and allow to cool slightly.

Remove pan with set Cranberry Layer from refrigerator. Ladle grapefruit mixture carefully over cranberry layer. Return pan to refrigerator and chill until fully set, several hours or overnight.

To serve, cut into desired shapes. Makes 18 to 24 jelly shots.

Screwdriver, Blood Orange

Difficulty: Easy
Recommended Pan: 1–pound loaf pan
(approximately 8" x 4" / 20 x 10 cm)

1 cup / 240 ml blood orange juice
  (strained to remove solids)

2 envelopes Knox gelatin

½ cup / 120 ml Cointreau

½ cup / 120 ml vodka

2 to 3 teaspoons Simple Syrup
  (see recipe on page 198) or
  agave nectar, if desired

A cocktail classic dressed for the holidays with seasonal blood orange juice and a dash of Cointreau. Of course, these jelly shots are just as nice year-round, prepared with regular orange juice. Note: With regular OJ you probably won't need the sweetener.

POUR THE BLOOD ORANGE juice into a medium saucepan and sprinkle with the gelatin. Allow the gelatin to soak for a minute or two. Heat over very low heat, stirring constantly, until gelatin is fully dissolved, about 5 minutes. Remove from the heat and stir in the Cointreau and the vodka. Taste and add simple syrup, if desired. Pour into loaf pan and refrigerate until fully set, several hours or overnight.

To serve, cut into desired shapes. Makes 18 to 24 jelly shots.

Sidecar

Difficulty: Intermediate
Recommended Pan: 9" × 9" / 23 × 23 cm
square or 9" / 23 cm round

¾ cup / 180 ml Lemon Syrup
   (see recipe on page 197)
½ cup / 120 ml water
3 envelopes Knox gelatin
1 cup / 240 ml brandy
1 cup / 240 ml Cointreau
Orange zest for garnish, if desired

Oh, how we love the Sidecar! This classic cocktail was reportedly concocted in the 1920s for a patron of a Paris bar—a patron commonly driven about in a motorcycle sidecar. We're not sure if that was before or after he downed a few of these.

COMBINE THE LEMON syrup and water in a medium saucepan and sprinkle with the gelatin. Allow the gelatin to soak for a minute or two. Heat over low heat, stirring constantly, until gelatin is dissolved, about 5 minutes. Remove from the heat and stir in the brandy and Cointreau. Pour into pan and refrigerate until set, several hours or overnight.

To serve, cut into desired shapes. Garnish each shot with orange zest, if desired. Makes 24 to 30 jelly shots.

Tequila Sunrise

Difficulty: Intermediate
Recommended Pan: 9" × 9" / 23 × 23 cm square or 9" / 23 cm round

Grenadine Layer

¾ cup / 180 ml grenadine
¼ cup / 60 ml water
1 envelope Knox gelatin

Orange Layer

1½ cups / 360 ml freshly
  squeezed orange juice (strained
  to remove solids)
3 envelopes Knox gelatin
1½ cups / 360 ml gold tequila

This jelly shot is hands down the fan favorite every time we make it. These can also be prepared using the Gradiated Layers technique (see Techniques section for details). If not using freshly squeezed orange juice, make sure your juice is top notch. If it's a bit flat or sour, just add a few tablespoons of frozen OJ concentrate to perk it up. Otherwise, you will have to cut back on the tequila to keep the flavors balanced, and that would be most unfortunate!

GRENADINE LAYER Pour the grenadine and water into a small saucepan and sprinkle with the gelatin. Allow the gelatin to soak for a minute or two. Heat over very low heat, stirring constantly, until gelatin is dissolved, about 5 minutes. Pour into pan and chill until fully set, about an hour. Prepare Orange Layer.

ORANGE LAYER Pour the orange juice into a medium saucepan and sprinkle with the gelatin. Allow the gelatin to soak for a minute or two. Heat over low heat, stirring constantly, until gelatin is dissolved, about 5 minutes. Remove from the heat and stir in the tequila. Allow mixture to cool slightly.

Remove pan with set Grenadine Layer from the refrigerator. Ladle the orange mixture carefully over the grenadine layer. Return to the refrigerator and chill until fully set, several hours or overnight.

To serve, cut into desired shapes. Makes 24 to 30 jelly shots.

Tom Collins

Difficulty: Intermediate
Recommended Pan: 1–pound loaf pan (approximately 8" x 4" / 20 x 10 cm) or hemisphere molds

⅔ cup / 165 ml club soda

⅔ cup / 165 ml Lemon Syrup
  (see recipe on page 197)

2 envelopes Knox gelatin

⅔ cup / 165 ml gin

½ teaspoon Simple Syrup
  (see recipe on page 198) or
  agave nectar, if desired

Orange slices and maraschino
  cherries for garnish, if desired

Made famous by the Planter's Hotel in St. Louis in the 1850s, the Tom Collins cocktail is very similar to the Gin Fizz. This jelly shot is beautiful when prepared in a hemisphere mold as shown, or in a flat pan, cut into squares and garnished with orange slivers and maraschino cherrries.

COMBINE THE CLUB soda and lemon syrup in a medium saucepan and sprinkle with the gelatin. Allow the gelatin to soak for a minute or two. Heat over low heat, stirring constantly, until gelatin is fully dissolved, about 5 minutes. Remove from the heat and stir in the gin. Taste and add simple syrup, if desired. Pour into loaf pan or molds and refrigerate until fully set, several hours or overnight.

To serve, cut into desired shapes or unmold shots. Garnish with slivers of orange and maraschino cherries. Makes 18 to 24 jelly shots.

Vodka Pink Lemonade

Difficulty: Easy

Recommended Pan: 1–pound loaf pan (approximately 8" x 4" / 20 x 10 cm)

⅔ cup / 165 ml frozen pink lemonade concentrate, thawed

⅔ cup / 165 ml water

2 envelopes Knox gelatin

⅔ cup / 165 ml vodka

Lemon zest for garnish, if desired

Drinking a Vodka Pink Lemonade (VPL for short) on the deck of Lord Fletcher's (a landmark Lake Minnetonka establishment) while watching flocks of pretty, oversized boats motor past is a summer tradition for Twin Cities locals and visitors alike. The Vodka Pink Lemonade jelly shot, like its cocktail inspiration, is refreshing and crisp and ever so tart on the tongue.

COMBINE THE LEMONADE concentrate and water in a medium saucepan. Strain to remove solids, and return to the saucepan. Sprinkle the mixture with the gelatin and allow to soak for a minute or two. Heat over low heat, stirring constantly, until gelatin is dissolved, about 5 minutes. Remove from the heat and stir in the vodka. Pour into loaf pan and refrigerate until set, several hours or overnight.

To serve, cut into desired shapes. Garnish with lemon zest, if desired. Makes 24 to 30 jelly shots.

Washington Apple

Difficulty: Easy
Recommended Pan: 1–pound loaf pan
(approximately 8" x 4" / 20 x 10 cm)

⅔ cup / 165 ml cranberry
   juice cocktail
2 envelopes Knox gelatin
⅔ cup / 165 ml Disaronno
   amaretto liqueur
⅔ cup / 165 ml Crown
   Royal whiskey
Green apple licorice whips
   for garnish

A thin slice of green apple licorice makes a cute and tasty "stem" detail. To make the stem, cut thin stem-like slices lengthwise from a licorice whip. To attach, poke a toothpick approximately ½ inch / 12 mm into each shot, wiggle gently to expand the hole, and insert the licorice "stem."

POUR THE CRANBERRY juice cocktail into a medium saucepan and sprinkle with the gelatin. Allow the gelatin to soak for a minute or two. Heat over low heat, stirring carefully and constantly, until gelatin is fully dissolved, about 5 minutes. Remove from the heat and stir in the amaretto and whiskey. Pour into loaf pan and refrigerate until fully set, several hours or overnight.

To serve, cut into squares and garnish with licorice. Makes 18 to 24 jelly shots.

White Chocolate Martini

Difficulty: Easy
Recommended Pan: 1–pound loaf pan
(approximately 8" × 4" / 20 × 10 cm)

"Ganache" Layer
½ cup / 120 ml chocolate milk
1 envelope Knox gelatin
½ cup / 120 ml Godiva dark
    chocolate liqueur

Martini Layer
½ cup / 120 ml milk (whole or 2%)
2 envelopes Knox gelatin
¼ cup / 60 ml Baileys Irish
    cream liqueur
½ cup / 120 ml Godiva white
    chocolate liqueur
½ cup / 120 ml vanilla-flavored vodka
Chocolate shavings for garnish

Smooth, creamy and delectable—this is the perfect dessert jelly shot.

"GANACHE" LAYER Pour the chocolate milk into a small saucepan and sprinkle with the gelatin. Allow the gelatin to soak for a minute or two. Heat over low heat, stirring constantly, until gelatin is fully dissolved, about 5 minutes. Remove from the heat and allow to cool slightly. Stir in chocolate liqueur. Pour mixture into loaf pan and refrigerate until fully set, one to two hours. Once mixture has set, prepare Martini Layer.

MARTINI LAYER Pour the milk into a medium saucepan and sprinkle with the gelatin. Allow the gelatin to soak for a minute or two. Heat over low heat, stirring constantly, until gelatin is fully dissolved, about 5 minutes. Remove from the heat and allow to cool slightly. Stir in the Baileys and white chocolate liqueur, and then the vodka.

Remove pan with set Ganache Layer from the refrigerator. Ladle Martini mixture carefully over the ganache layer. Return pan to the refrigerator and chill until fully set, several hours or overnight.

To serve, cut into desired shapes and garnish with chocolate shavings. Makes 18 to 24 jelly shots.

Whiskey Sour

Difficulty: Intermediate

Recommended Pan: 1–pound loaf pan (approximately 8" × 4" / 20 × 10 cm)

1½ cups / 360 ml Lemon Syrup
  (see recipe on page 197)

2 teaspoons granulated sugar

2½ envelopes Knox gelatin

1 cup / 240 ml whiskey

Maraschino cherries for garnish,
  if desired

T he most popular member of the beloved "sour family" of cocktails.

COMBINE THE LEMON syrup and sugar in a medium saucepan and sprinkle with the gelatin. Allow the gelatin to soak for a minute or two. Heat over low heat, stirring constantly, until gelatin is fully dissolved, about 5 minutes. Remove from the heat and add the whiskey, stirring well to blend. Pour into loaf pan and refrigerate until fully set, several hours or overnight.

To serve, cut into desired shapes. Garnish each shot with a maraschino cherry segment, if desired. Makes 24 to 32 jelly shots.

White Russian

Difficulty: Advanced
Recommended Pan: 1–pound loaf pan
(approximately 8" × 4" / 20 × 10 cm)

Coffee Layer
½ cup / 120 ml brewed strong coffee
  or espresso
1 ½ envelopes Knox gelatin
½ cup / 120 ml Kahlúa coffee liqueur
½ cup / 120 ml vodka

Milk Layer
½ cup / 120 ml milk (whole or 2%)
½ envelope Knox gelatin

Delicious, decadent, and dessert-y, these jelly shots are lovely prepared in two simple layers per the instructions below, or for the dramatic presentation shown here, you can use the Embedded Shapes method, cutting the set milk layer into small rectangles before placing into the coffee layer (see Techniques section for details).

COFFEE LAYER Pour the coffee into a small saucepan and sprinkle with the gelatin. Allow the gelatin to soak for a minute or two. Heat over very low heat until gelatin is dissolved, stirring constantly, about 5 minutes. Remove from the heat and add the Kahlúa and vodka, stirring well to blend. Pour into loaf pan and refrigerate until fully set, at least an hour. Prepare Milk Layer.

MILK LAYER Pour the milk into a small saucepan and sprinkle with the gelatin. Allow the gelatin to soak for a few minutes. Heat over very low heat until gelatin is dissolved, stirring constantly, about 5 minutes. Remove from the heat and allow to cool slightly.

Remove set Coffee Layer from the refrigerator. Ladle milk mixture carefully over set coffee layer in pan. Return pan to the refrigerator and chill until fully set, several hours or overnight.

To serve, cut into desired shapes. Makes 18 to 24 jelly shots.

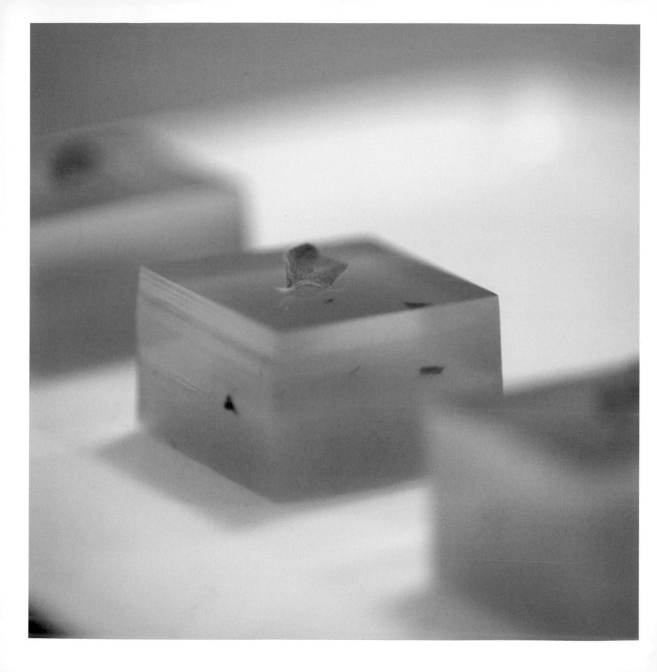

Non Alcoholic
Options

Apples and Oranges

Difficulty: Advanced
Recommended Pan: Two 1–pound loaf pans (approximately 8" × 4" / 20 × 10 cm) and two mini loaf pans (approximately 6" × 3" / 15 × 7.5 cm each) for setting the shapes

1½ cups / 360 ml orange juice
½ cup / 120 ml orange soda
4 envelopes Knox gelatin, divided
2 cups / 480 ml apple juice

A juicy and refreshing delight for kids of all ages. Prepare as directed below, or simply as a two-layer jelly shot. This shot works well with any two contrasting-color juices.

COMBINE THE ORANGE juice and orange soda in a medium saucepan and sprinkle with 2 envelopes of gelatin. Allow the gelatin to soak for a minute or two. Heat over low heat, stirring constantly, until the gelatin is dissolved, about 5 minutes. Set aside.

Pour the apple juice into a separate medium saucepan and sprinkle with the remaining 2 envelopes of gelatin. Allow the gelatin to soak for a minute or two. Heat over low heat, stirring constantly, until the gelatin is dissolved, about 5 minutes.

Pour ½ cup / 120 ml of the apple mixture into a mini loaf pan. Pour ½ cup / 120 ml of the orange mixture into another mini loaf pan. Place the mini loaf pans in the freezer, making sure to keep them level. Pour the remaining apple and orange mixtures into two separate standard loaf pans, and set aside.

The mixtures in the mini loaf pans should set in 15 to 20 minutes. Watch carefully to avoid freezing. (If a few ice crystals do form, simply remove the pans from the freezer and allow to warm up on the countertop for a few minutes before proceeding.)

When set. cut circular shapes in the apple and orange gelatin with a small round cookie cutter. Arrange the apple circles in the reserved orange mixture, one by one. Repeat with the orange circles in the reserved apple mixture. Carefully transfer the pans to the refrigerator and chill until fully set, several hours or overnight.

To serve, cut into desired shapes. Makes 36 to 42 large jelly shots.

Pom Cherry Lemonade

Difficulty: Advanced
Recommended Pan: 1–pound loaf pan
(approximately 8" x 4" / 20 x 10 cm)

1⅓ cups / 315 ml Lemon Syrup
  (see recipe on page 197), divided
⅓ cup / 75 ml diet lemon-lime soda
2 envelopes Knox gelatin, divided
⅓ cup / 75 ml cherry-pomegranate
  juice

Beloved by totalers tee and total, this zingy jelly shot may be prepared as illustrated using the Checkerboard technique (see Techniques section for details). Instructions for a simple layered shot are below.

COMBINE ⅔ CUP / 165 ml lemon syrup and the lemon-lime soda in a small saucepan and sprinkle with one envelope of the gelatin. Allow the gelatin to soak for a minute or two. Heat over low heat, stirring constantly, until the gelatin is dissolved, about 5 minutes. Pour into a pan and refrigerate until fully set, about an hour.

Combine the remaining lemon syrup and the juice in a small saucepan and sprinkle with remaining envelope of gelatin. Allow the gelatin to soak for a minute or two. Heat over low heat, stirring constantly, until the gelatin is dissolved, about 5 minutes. Allow mixture to cool slightly. Pour over chilled layer and refrigerate until fully set, preferably overnight.

To serve, cut into desired shapes. Makes 18 to 24 jelly shots.

Shirley Temple

Difficulty: Intermediate
Recommended Pan: 1–pound loaf pan (approximately 8" x 4" / 20 x 10 cm)

1¼ cups / 360 ml diet lemon-lime soda

½ cup / 120 ml Pomegranate Syrup (see recipe on page 198)

2 envelopes Knox gelatin

Maraschino cherries for garnish, if desired

Prepare with a gradient layer (see Techniques section for details), separating the soda and homemade grenadine into two layers using 1½ envelopes gelatin and ½ envelope gelatin, respectively, as shown, or simply combine all the ingredients (as directed below) for a cherry-hued sweet treat. The homemade grenadine here adds a touch of pleasant tartness.

COMBINE THE SODA and the pomegranate syrup in a medium saucepan and sprinkle with the gelatin. Allow the gelatin to soak for a minute or two. Heat over low heat, stirring constantly, until gelatin is dissolved, about 5 minutes. Pour into loaf pan and refrigerate until set, several hours or overnight.

To serve, cut into shapes. Garnish with maraschino cherry segments, if desired. Makes 18 to 24 jelly shots.

Lavender Lemonade

Difficulty: Intermediate

Recommended Pan: 1–pound loaf pan
(approximately 8" x 4" / 20 x 10 cm)

1½ cups / 360 ml Lemon Syrup
  (see recipe on page 197)
½ cup / 120 ml diet lemon-lime soda
1 tablespoon dried lavender
  (food grade)
2 envelopes Knox gelatin
Edible flowers for garnish, if desired

The addition of lavender adds a touch of sophistication to a mocktail jelly shot. Experiment using any of your favorite aromatics, such as marjoram or basil, in place of the lavender.

COMBINE THE LEMON syrup, soda, and lavender in a medium saucepan and sprinkle with the gelatin. Allow the gelatin to soak for a minute or two. Heat over low heat, stirring constantly, until gelatin is fully dissolved, about 5 minutes. Remove from the heat and strain to remove lavender. Pour strained mixture into loaf pan and refrigerate until set, several hours or overnight.

To serve, cut into desired shapes and garnish with edible flowers, if desired. Makes 16 to 24 jelly shots.

Mimosa,
Orange Tarragon Cucumber

Difficulty: Intermediate

Recommended Pan: 1–pound loaf pan (approximately 8" x 4" / 20 x 10 cm)

Implements: Cocktail shaker and cocktail muddler

Orange Layer

1 (1-inch / 2.5 cm) piece cucumber, coarsely chopped

1 large sprig fresh tarragon

1 cup / 240 ml freshly squeezed orange juice (strained to remove solids)

6 ice cubes

1 envelope Knox gelatin

Sparkling Juice Layer

1 cup / 240 ml Meier's sparkling spumante, or other non alcoholic sparkling juice

1 envelope Knox gelatin

¼ teaspoon finely chopped fresh tarragon, if desired

Fresh tarragon leaves for garnish

This chic and tasty non alcoholic jelly shot makes teetotaling a distinctly grown-up pleasure. Freshly squeezed orange juice is preferred for this recipe, as the juice is the star of the show. However, juice from concentrate may be used, provided it is top notch—if it is a little flat or sour, add a few teaspoons of frozen orange juice concentrate or a light sweetener, such as agave nectar, to perk it up.

ORANGE LAYER Muddle together the cucumber and tarragon in the bottom of the cocktail shaker. Add the orange juice and ice cubes. Shake well and strain; you should have 1 cup / 240 ml of liquid.

Pour the orange liquid into a small saucepan and sprinkle with the gelatin. Allow the gelatin to soak for a minute or two. Heat on low, stirring constantly, until gelatin is fully dissolved, about 5 minutes. Pour into loaf pan and chill until fully set, about an hour. Prepare Sparkling Juice Layer.

SPARKLING JUICE LAYER Pour the sparkling juice into a small saucepan and sprinkle with the gelatin. Allow the gelatin to soak for a minute or two. Heat on low, stirring constantly, until gelatin is fully dissolved, about 5 minutes. Remove from the heat and stir in the chopped tarragon, if using.

Remove the set Orange Layer from the refrigerator. Ladle the sparkling juice mixture carefully over the set orange layer in pan. Return pan to the refrigerator and chill until fully set, several hours or overnight.

To serve, cut into desired shapes. Garnish each shot with a small tarragon leaf. Makes 18 to 24 jelly shots.

Mimosa,
Grapefruit Marjoram Ginger

Difficulty: Intermediate

Recommended Pan: 1–pound loaf pan (approximately 8" x 4" / 20 x 10 cm)

Implements: Cocktail shaker and cocktail muddler

Grapefruit Layer

1 (¾-inch / 2 cm) piece fresh ginger, coarsely chopped

1 large sprig fresh marjoram

1 cup freshly squeezed grapefruit juice (strained to remove solids)

6 ice cubes

1 tablespoon honey or agave nectar

1 envelope Knox gelatin

Sparkling Juice Layer

1 cup Meier's sparkling spumante, or other non alcoholic sparkling juice

1 envelope Knox gelatin

¼ teaspoon finely chopped fresh marjoram, if desired

Fresh marjoram leaves for garnish

A nother take on our non alcoholic Mimosa theme, using three subtly spicy flavors as a foil for sparkling juice.

GRAPEFRUIT LAYER Muddle the ginger and marjoram in the bottom of the cocktail shaker. Add the grapefruit juice and ice cubes. Shake well and strain; you should have 1 cup / 240 ml of liquid.

Pour the strained grapefruit liquid and honey into a small saucepan and sprinkle with the gelatin. Allow the gelatin to soak for a minute or two. Heat on low, stirring constantly, until gelatin is fully dissolved, about 5 minutes. Pour the mixture into loaf pan and chill until set, about an hour. Prepare Sparkling Juice Layer.

SPARKLING JUICE LAYER Pour the sparkling juice into a small saucepan and sprinkle with the gelatin. Allow the gelatin to soak for a minute or two. Heat on low, stirring constantly, until gelatin is fully dissolved, about 5 minutes. Add chopped marjoram, if desired.

Remove set Grapefruit Layer from refrigerator. Ladle sparkling juice mixture carefully over the set grapefruit layer in pan. Return to refrigerator and chill until fully set, several hours or overnight.

To serve, cut into desired shapes and garnish each shot with a marjoram leaf. Makes 18 to 24 jelly shots.

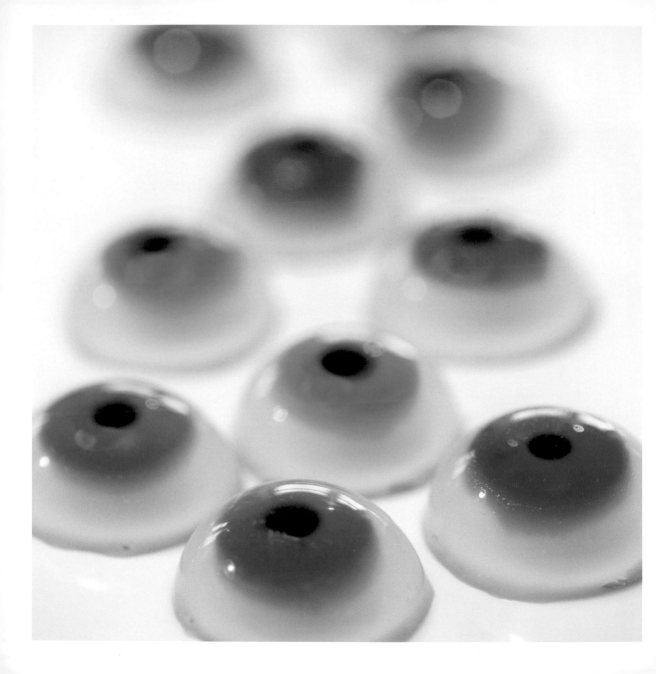

Passion Fruit Sparkler

Difficulty: Advanced
Recommended Pan: 9" × 9" / 23 × 23 cm square or 9" / 23 cm round

1½ cups / 360 ml passion fruit nectar

1½ cups / 360 ml diet lemon-lime soda

Splash of freshly squeezed lemon or lime juice, if desired

3 envelopes Knox gelatin

These are delicious prepared as a simple shot, but ghoulishly delightful prepared as shown with the Eyeball technique (see Techniques section for details).

COMBINE THE PASSION fruit nectar and soda in a medium saucepan. Add the lemon or lime juice, if desired. Sprinkle with the gelatin and allow gelatin to soak for a minute or two. Heat over low heat, stirring constantly, until gelatin is dissolved, about 5 minutes. Pour into pan and refrigerate until fully set, several hours or overnight.

To serve, cut into desired shapes. Makes 24 to 32 jelly shots.

"Pom's" Cup

Difficulty: Intermediate

Recommended Pan: 1–pound loaf pan (approximately 8" x 4" / 20 x 10 cm)

Implements: Cocktail shaker and cocktail muddler

1 (1-inch / 2.5 cm) piece cucumber, coarsely chopped

4 strawberries

Large mint sprig

¾ cup / 180 ml water

6 ice cubes

¾ cup / 180 ml ginger ale

2 tablespoons Lemon Syrup (see recipe on page 197) or frozen lemonade concentrate

½ cup / 120 ml Pomegranate Syrup (see recipe on page 198)

2 envelopes Knox gelatin

Slivers of fruit and mint for garnish, if desired

Those who love the Pimm's Cup but find themselves unable to indulge will enjoy this virgin version of the popular cocktail, in which pomegranate stands in for the Pimm's No. 1 liqueur. Prepare as shown with a gradient layer (see Gradient Layers in the Techniques section), separating the ingredients into two layers: one layer including the lemon syrup, ginger ale, and fruit liquid, and one layer with the grenadine, using 1½ envelopes gelatin and ½ envelope gelatin, respectively. Or simply combine all the ingredients per the instructions below.

IN A COCKTAIL shaker, muddle together the cucumber, strawberries, and mint. Add the water and ice cubes and shake vigorously. Strain liquid through a fine mesh strainer to remove any solids. You should have ¾ cup / 180 ml liquid. Set aside.

Combine the ginger ale, lemon syrup, and pomegranate syrup in a small saucepan and sprinkle with the gelatin. Allow the gelatin to soak for a minute or two. Heat over low heat, stirring constantly, until gelatin is dissolved, about 5 minutes. Allow to cool slightly. Add the reserved fruit liquid, stirring well to blend. Pour mixture into loaf pan, and chill until fully set, several hours or overnight.

To serve, cut into desired shapes and garnish with fruit and mint slices, if desired. Makes 18 to 24 jelly shots.

Syrup
Recipes

LIKE MIXERS FOR A LIQUID

cocktail, the following recipes comprise bases for many of our jelly shots. Although some recipes are unique to our jelly shots, have no fear—any unused syrup will also work brilliantly in your liquid cocktail creations. The syrups will keep for several days refrigerated in a tightly sealed container and for a week or two with the addition of a dash of high proof spirits such as vodka.

Although we emphasize using fresh ingredients whenever possible, we have also included some purchased "short cuts" that work just as well in a pinch.

Bitters Syrup

1½ cups / 360 ml water
1 cup / 200 g granulated sugar
9 tablespoons angostura bitters

Combine all ingredients in a medium saucepan. Heat over medium-high heat until mixture boils, stirring occasionally. Remove from the heat and allow to cool to room temperature.

Chai Syrup

1½ cups / 360 ml water
1 cup / 200 g granulated sugar
8 tea bags chai spice tea (Stash brand works well)

Combine all ingredients in a medium saucepan. Heat over medium heat until sugar is dissolved, about 5 minutes. The tea should be brewed, and the mixture will be very dark brown. Remove from the heat and strain syrup through fine mesh to remove any tea leaf fragments. Allow the syrup to cool to room temperature.

Lemon Syrup

1½ cups / 360 ml water
1 cup / 200 g granulated sugar
4 medium lemons, each cut into 8 wedges

Combine all ingredients in a medium saucepan. Muddle the lemon wedges. Bring to a rolling boil over medium heat. Reduce heat to low and simmer for 5 minutes. Remove from the heat and strain immediately. Allow the syrup to cool to room temperature.

SHORT CUT: A 50-50 mix of frozen lemonade concentrate and water may be substituted for Lemon Syrup in any recipe. Make sure to strain to remove any lemon pulp!

Lime Syrup

1½ cups / 360 ml water
1 cup / 200 g granulated sugar
4 medium limes, each cut into 8 wedges
¼ cup / 60 ml Rose's lime juice

Combine water, sugar, and limes in a medium saucepan. Muddle the limes. Bring to a rolling boil over medium heat. Reduce heat to low and simmer for 5 minutes. Remove from the heat and strain immediately. Stir in the Rose's lime juice. Allow the syrup to cool to room temperature.

SHORT CUT: A 50-50 mix of frozen limeade concentrate and water may be substituted for Lime Syrup in any recipe. Make sure to strain to remove any lime pulp!

Key Lime Syrup

Prepare Lime Syrup recipe, above, substituting a 1-pound / 455 g bag of Key limes, halved, for the regular limes.

Mojito Syrup

1½ cups / 360 ml water
1 cup / 200 g granulated sugar
2 limes, quartered
¼ cup / 60 ml Rose's lime juice
1 cup / 20 g mint leaves

Combine water, sugar, quartered limes, Rose's lime juice and mint in a medium saucepan and bring to a boil; reduce heat to low and simmer for five minutes. Remove pan from heat, and allow mixture to cool to room temperature before straining.

Pomegranate Syrup (Homemade Grenadine)

½ cup / 100 g granulated sugar
½ cup / 120 ml water
1 cup / 240 ml pomegranate juice

Combine the sugar, water, and ½ cup / 120 ml pomegranate juice in a small saucepan. Heat over medium heat until sugar is dissolved, stirring constantly. Remove from the heat and stir in remaining pomegranate juice. Allow the syrup to cool to room temperature.

Strawberry Syrup

1 (12-ounce / 340 g) jar seedless strawberry jam
1½ cups / 360 ml water

Combine jam and water in a medium saucepan. Heat over low heat until jam is dissolved. Remove from the heat and allow to cool to room temperature. Transfer syrup to a jar and refrigerate.

SHORT CUT: A high quality purchased strawberry syrup, such as Monin brand, may be substituted for strawberry syrup in any recipe.

Simple Syrup (Bar Syrup)

1 cup / 200 g granulated sugar
1 cup / 240 ml water

Combine sugar and water in a medium saucepan. Heat over medium heat until the sugar is dissolved, about 5 minutes. Remove from the heat and allow to cool to room temperature.

Resources

WE ARE OFTEN ASKED ABOUT what types of spirits work best in jelly shots. Our response is always that the best jelly shots are made with the same high-quality spirits that you enjoy in liquid cocktails. For reference, we have listed some our favorite, widely available imbibables, as well as sources for the serving dishes and tableware to complement your jelly shots.

VODKA: Kettle One is a great all-around. Belvedere is wonderful for sweeter shots. Hangar One makes wonderful fruit flavored vodka.

www.ketelone.com

www.belvederevodka.com

www.hangarone.com

GIN: Sorry gin traditionalists, but we are big proponents of Hendrick's Gin, which is lovely in jelly shots and absolutely vital for both the Negroni and the Aviation jelly shots. As far as old-school gin goes, we tested and were quite fond of Bombay Sapphire in the Gin & Juice, Tom Collins, Gimlet, Bee's Knees, and other gin-based recipes.

www.hendricksgin.com

www.bombaysapphire.com

BOURBON: We used Maker's Mark bourbon for the bourbon-based recipes herein, but there are lots of really nice bourbons available these days. Use what's in your liquor cabinet. www.makersmark.com

CHOCOLATE LIQUEURS: Godiva's White Chocolate and Chocolate liqueurs are wonderful, and handle gelatinization better than the white and dark crème de cacaos that are used in their classic cocktail inspirations. www.godiva.com/beyond_chocolate/entry.aspx

COINTREAU: Hail to the king of all orange liqueurs—heartily citrusy, but with mellow, blendable characteristics. We love it so and wouldn't think of using another. http://www.cointreau.com

MOLDS: Kerekes stocks a large variety of high-quality, affordable, flexible silicone molds in a multitude of shapes and sizes.
www.BakeDeco.com
Showroom: 6103-15th Avenue
Brooklyn, New York
718-232-7044

PLATTERS, PLATES, AND OTHER DISPLAY ITEMS:

CRATE & BARREL: No surprise to anyone that Crate & Barrel is absolutely brilliant for reasonably priced white and glass open-stock plates, platters, and tasting spoons.
http://www.crateandbarrel.com

COST PLUS WORLD MARKET: Also a great source; carries small plates and platters designed specifically for tasting menus that are ideal for presenting jelly shots at smaller gatherings.
http://www.worldmarket.com

CRUCIAL DETAIL: Purveyor of nothing short of fantastic avant-garde tableware to the fabled Alinea restaurant in Chicago, and now to the Jelly Shot Test Kitchen (and you!). The "craters" platter used for the Sidecar photograph and the tiny ceramic "sectional" pedestals in the Pretty in Pink flight photographs were purchased from Crucial Detail.
http://www.crucialdetail.com

SUR LA TABLE: Wonderful selection of open-stock white plates, amazing long platters, and very nice smaller, narrow platters as well.
http://surlatable.com

Acknowledgments

For starters, thanks to the dedicated team at Running Press. In particular, I would like to thank my editor, Jennifer Kasius, not only for believing in such a unique concept but also for her extraordinarily patient, spot-on editing, and designer Frances Soo Ping Chow who exhibited such skill in pulling all the elements together.

My sister, Amy Webster, whose photographs first breathed life into the jelly shot concept, deserves a wealth of gratitude for her vision and efforts.

Thanks to Kevin Johnston of Johnston Imaging for his inspired work in the home stretch of the project, and for always making my images look their best.

A million thanks to *Jelly Shot Test Kitchen*'s testers, including: Chad & Kate Ford; Mike & Kerri Hiniker, Mary Kelley, Doug Miller & Heidi Henderson, Eric Norman, and the many others who sampled along the way—not only was your feedback integral, your tireless enthusiasm for jelly shots was always appreciated.

Last but not least, thanks to *Jelly Shot Test Kitchen*'s counsel, Helene Freeman, for her insight, wisdom and uncanny knack for being 100% right.

Index

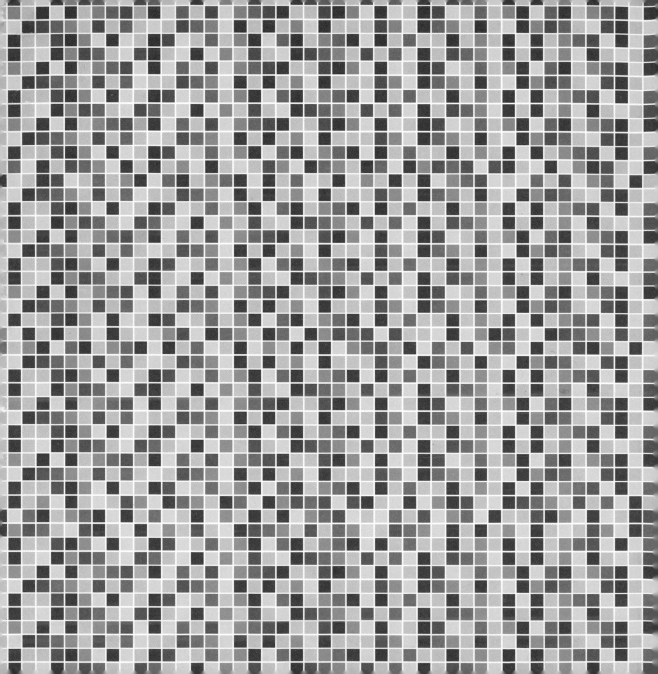